INSIGHT COMPACT GUIDES

Devon
& EXMOOR

GREAT LITTLE GUIDES

Compact Guide: Devon is the ideal quick-reference guide to this much-loved part of England. It tells you all you need to know about its attractions, from historic Exeter to bustling Brixham, from the beaches of Woolacombe to the beautiful Doone Valley.

This is just one title in *Apa Publications'* new series of pocket-sized, easy-to-use guidebooks intended for the independent-minded traveller. *Compact Guides* pride themselves on being up-to-date and authoritative. They are in essence mini travel encyclopedias, designed to be comprehensive yet portable, as well as readable and reliable.

GW00691621

RIVER LINK

Star Attractions

An instant reference to some of Devon's most popular tourist attractions to help you on your way.

Exeter Cathedral p17

Torquay p25

Dartington Hall p30

Dartmouth p31

Morwellham p37

Dartmoor p38

Clovelly p51

The North Coast p53

Brixham Harbour p27

Lynton Cliff Railway p55

Tarr Steps p57

Devon
& EXMOOR

Introduction

Places

Culture

Leisure

Practical Information

Devon – Village England

Opposite: Clovelly

At 75 miles (120km) deep and 73 miles (116km) wide, Devon is the third largest county in the UK. Approached by land, its initial impact is almost unnoticed, but climbing hedges, narrowing lanes and lazy tractors soon impose a Devonian calm. Going too fast? Then have a cream tea.

Topography and Climate

Devon is a county of great seascapes, with extensive coastlines both north and south, giving rise to tremendous cliff scenery (the highest in England) punctuated by equally fine coves and beaches. In between the two coasts is what is often referred to as 'deepest Devon' – a land of river valleys and leafy lanes. Despite its two big cities, Plymouth and Exeter, this is fundamentally a county of villages, most of which haven't changed for centuries.

Devon man

Deepest Devon

Deepest Devon is a pastoral land, traditionally dedicated to agriculture, although the quality of the soil has never been such to produce the super-farms that are found elsewhere in the country. Most farmers practise the ley system, where land is used for crops for 2–3 years, and then given over to pasture for 7–10 years. Accordingly, dairy and sheep farming is prevalent.

The grass is a deep lush green for good reason. Dartmoor, which reaches 2,000ft (600m), is the highest stretch of land in the south of England, and Exmoor is not far behind; the two of them each receive up to 90 inches (230cm) of rain per year, five times the amount which falls on London. Such rainfall spawns numerous fast-flowing rivers that run off the moors to water many a Devon valley.

Picture-book prettiness

But while the moors create their own micro-climate ('Wet and boggy/Cold and soggy/Deep and smelly/Pulls off my welly' is one contemporary description of Dartmoor), other areas are remarkably balmy. Torbay, which calls itself the English Riviera, holds the record for the warmest and sunniest days in the UK thanks to its southerly and sheltered location. Average September temperatures here are 17.5 °C (63.5°F), while Nice is only two degrees warmer at 19.7 °C (67.5°F). Along the southeastern slopes are several vineyards, making the most of the extra sun.

The South Devon coast has a variety of very safe anchorages, creeks and estuaries which in their day attracted traders and ship-builders. Crusades and *Mayflower* pilgrims set off from these southern shores, but now that world shipping concentrates on greater distances and fewer ports, Devon is largely ignored other than at Plymouth, where the Royal Navy is particularly active. Elsewhere the vacancy created by the end of merchant shipping

5

Yachts in Dartmouth harbour

has been filled by leisure boating, and many a former port now harbours a new marina, from where sea-going is mostly done at weekends.

The northern coastline is far more inhospitable than the south, and shares with Cornwall the reputation for wrecks and wreckers. Harbours have to be particularly well situated – such as at Ilfracombe and Watermouth – to survive. The former pier at Westward Ho! and quay at Hartland are two examples of how the sea can sweep away the handiwork of man.

Devonians

According to the 1991 census, 1,009,950 people live in Devon, with the greatest concentration in the warmer south. The traditional Devon character is largely one of cheerful independence. Generations of owner-occupying small farmers have produced a population of tidy conservatives (with a small c), who like to do their own thing and not be interfered with by a government which still seems a long way away. Recreation is a scrumpy in the pub and fox-hunting at the weekend; luxury is a new car every couple of years.

Meet the locals

But don't be misled: just because an old gent has a ruddy complexion and a thick country accent, it doesn't mean he hasn't seen the world. Indeed, Dartmoor folk are meant to be particularly wordly wise: 'You scratch my back, I'll steal your purse' runs the saying.

Of course, there are typical folk remedies along the lines of 'If your child has whooping cough, put him to sleep in a shed with a sheep', and rural eccentrics such as Parson Froude of Knowstone, who was hardly ever seen in church but spent his career hunting, shooting and fishing. Parson Froude kept his own pack of hounds, but shouldn't be confused with the altogether more conscientious Parson Jack Russell of Swimbridge, who bred the terrier that bears his name.

Devon was the birthplace of adventurers Drake, Grenville and Raleigh, and many Devonians have travelled widely in the merchant navy or in the armed forces, both of which have a strong presence through the county.

Wages and income levels are low compared to the national average, but Devonians don't complain: they're usually more concerned about the weather or the prospects for the darts team, next week's fair or last week's debacle at Plymouth Argyle. Local pubs play a key role in these communities – as breweries have found out to their chagrin when they've tried to modernise their properties in order to move them upmarket.

Devon has a small, loyal aristocracy. Family names such as Acland, Chichester, Carew and Pole crop up regularly, but other than the Courtenays of Powderham, near Exeter, and the Aclands at Killerton, few of the country estates were of the size and wealth attained elsewhere in the country. The pickings in Devon were simply not rich enough, and distances too great from the court to achieve the sort of influence that allows the garnering of great wealth.

These few Devonian families have showed great tenacity, however, and although the National Trust may be in possession of the family seat, family members are often still in residence either in part of the house or elsewhere on the estate.

In Devon, local doesn't necessarily mean parochial, but it certainly means an emphasis on tradition and independence. After all, it was a Devon village (Sampford Courtenay) which rose against the gentry after the Reformation to demand a return to the Latin of the old prayer book. For such presumption, the rebellion was mercilessly repressed.

Cockington village fete

The continued emphasis on tradition is reflected in a wide range of annual events, some of which date back so far into the past that their genesis has been forgotten. These include the tar barrel ceremony of Ottery St Mary, where local men hoist blazing barrels onto their shoulders, originally symbolising protestant reaction to the gunpowder plot; Beer regatta, where local fishermen race from one side of the bay to the other, using every form of unorthodox distraction short of ramming each other, which hearkens back to smuggling days and trying to outrun customs; Widecombe Fair and the Ashburton Ale Tasting and Bread Weighing Ceremony, both of which date back to the days when Dartmoor played host to hard-living tin and copper miners; and the hot pennies ceremony of Honiton, where heated pennies were thrown by sadistic gentry who liked to see street urchins burn their fingers.

The Economy

Some 18 percent of Devonians are self-employed, compared with a national average of 12 percent. Big businesses are rare; 90 percent of employers have a payroll of fewer than 25 people, and wage levels as a whole are 12 percent below the national average at £312 per week for a male worker. In terms of numbers of employees the largest sectors are services and distribution, followed by banking, manufacturing and engineering, with agriculture, forestry and fishing some way down the list.

The industrial revolution passed Devon by, which is why the region's landscape and infrastructure have changed comparatively little since Domesday. Local textile mills were common in the south, where a combination of plenty of sheep, fast-running water (to turn the mill's waterwheels) and nearby ports helped keep what was essentially a cottage industry afloat despite the competition from the huge textile mills of the north.

Exeter old port

Farming still thrives

Mining was a boom industry from the 13th to 19th century, particularly on Dartmoor (tin) and around Tavistock (copper) but these days only ball clay is mined in any quantity. Manufacturing is limited to the Plymouth and to a lesser extent Exeter areas and a few light industries scattered county-wide, taking advantage of relatively low wage levels and overheads.

Financial services are strong in Exeter, particularly along the rural-sounding but splendid-looking Southernhay. Fishing is still an active industry on the south coast, where some 600 of the county's 1,250 fishermen are based at Brixham.

The core of Devon's quiet independence has always been farming, but these are essentially traditionalist small farmers (the vast majority of Devon's 11,000 farms are between 50–100 hectares/120–250 acres), who've found it hard to compete with the growing European market and the supermarket culture. Tourism – bed & breakfast, pony trekking, etc – has thrown a lifeline to many of them.

The armed forces have a significant impact on the region, with several bases, firing ranges on Dartmoor and a strong fleet presence at Plymouth.

Tourism

Some 3.5 million people visit Devon every year, with the majority heading to the south, where Torbay accommodates a third of them. The industry is worth £310 million in direct income, and is considered to be the largest single revenue earner for the county.

Holidaymakers discovered the south coast first, with Exmouth becoming a resort as early as the 18th century. Torquay swiftly followed, partly as a result of the Napoleonic Wars. Physicians on navy ships sheltering in Tor Bay realised how mild the local climate was, and started to recommend the bay to their private patients. This, combined with the fact that much of Europe was out of bounds to the British thanks to prolonged warring with France, gave Devon tourism a hefty boost.

The arrival of the railway from the 1840s onward dictated how this tourism spread, and some places have dwindled in importance following the removal of rail services in the 1950s and '60s. In North Devon, for example, there were once six railway routes; now there is only one. Resort towns such as Ilfracombe will never quite recover the atmosphere of their boom times.

Fortunately, a couple of the most scenic railway routes have been preserved by local societies (Buckfastleigh to Torquay and Paignton to Kingswear are two examples), while other disused track beds have been adapted to walkways such as the Tarka Trail, which runs between Dartmoor and Exmoor.

Beside the seaside

The arrival of the motor car moved the emphasis away from the beach resorts and opened up the countryside, spawning innumerable wildlife sanctuaries, farm centres and nature parks, and attracting a different sort of visitor. Today the county has a huge number of holiday cottages for rent, most of them 'in deepest Devon'.

On the verge

Dartmoor and Exmoor

Devon's two National Parks are storehouses of ancient monuments and increasingly rare wildlife. Dartmoor, which has been largely left alone by recent civilisation, has accordingly turned up some good evidence of early man. But don't be confused by the marks left by tin mining, such as the granite trackway near Haytor. This was built in the 19th century to serve the granite mines, although it looks as old as the hills. Exmoor also bears some evidence of Stone Age habitation, although more extensive farming has wiped much of the former landscape clean.

The moors are good at generating legends. The Hound of the Baskervilles lingers around Dartmoor, while the Beast of Exmoor continues to stalk the uplands and elude photographers and hunters. Exmoor has the largest herd of wild red deer outside Scotland, while Dartmoor ponies are ubiquitous. Otters are holding their own in areas of Exmoor, but rarely seen by the casual visitor. Adders, too, are relatively common, but equally rarely seen.

Both landscapes, despite being in the management of the National Parks, are still largely privately owned, and continuing access and the preservation of these precious environments depends on good relationships between all parties. For the individual walker, that means keeping to established footpaths, restraining dogs, closing gates and leaving behind nothing except footprints – and only leaving those in the right places.

9

Dartmoor in winter

Historical Highlights

c400,000BC First Stone Age people cross into region of Devon.

c30,000BC Date of first proven human settlement of Devon, from a teenager's jawbone found in Kent's Cavern, Torquay.

c18,000BC Hyenas, cave bears and mammoths still at large in Devon, again according to fossilised remains found in Kent's Cavern.

2500BC onwards Dartmoor, warmer than it is today, is first used by Bronze Age man for ritual and burial sites, and then latterly is cultivated. Beaker folk (so-called because of their pottery) start to settle around Exmoor. The Dumnonii tribe starts to make Devon its home.

c750BC Arrival of the Iron Age, typified by warlike tribes and the creation of hill forts such as Cow Castle near Simonsbath. Around 55 such forts have been found in Devon.

80–85BC Isca Dumnoniorum (Exeter) founded.

49AD Romans make a base at Seaton, later transferring to Exeter. They complete the Exeter City Wall by 200AD, and send sorties further west, but make no substantial settlement, although a Roman fort has been found at Okehampton. Eventually they leave Devon and then England to defend the core of their crumbling empire.

2nd–7th centuries The Dark Ages, the time of Arthurian legend.

c680 St Boniface is born in Crediton, and spreads Christianity locally and into Europe. Devon's first cathedral is built in Crediton in the 10th century. Saxon invasions create the kingdom of Wessex. In 710 King Ine defeats the British and builds a fortress at Taunton. Monasteries are established, including Tavistock in 974.

876 and 1003 Danes capture Exeter, which with Lydford, Totnes and Pilton (now a district of Barnstaple) were the only official burghs of Devon.

1050 The diocesan centre is transferred from Crediton to Exeter, and the cathedral is begun.

1066 Norman invasion of Britain under William the Conqueror. Exeter submits. The first Norman sheriff of Devon was Baldwin de Brionne, from Courtenay near Paris. He built the first Okehampton castle in 1068, and his descendants, the Courtenays, Earls of Devon, still live at Powderham Castle near Exeter.

1086 Domesday Book lists 1,170 place names in Devon, and gives the county a population of 60,000.

1147 and 1190 Second and Third Crusades leave from Dartmouth.

1152 Henry II marries Eleanor of Aquitaine, in Southwest France. The increased trade between Britain and France greatly benefits Devon's ports, because of their proximity to that region of France.

1196 Torre Abbey, Torquay, is founded.

1239 The Forest of Dartmoor is officially established as a hunting ground, and administered from Lydford. Ashburton becomes the first stannary (tin-mining) town in 1285.

1272 Customs duties introduced for the first time, thus marking the beginning of smuggling, a business to which Devon – with its creeks and coves – proves to be admirably suited.

c1350–70 Black Death sweeps through Devon. In Totnes alone 600 people die, leaving it a ghost town with grass growing in the street.

1404 Dartmouth invaded by rampaging Bretons, who quickly left again. The cloth industry is at its most successful.

1536–39 Dissolution of the monasteries by Henry VIII. Torre Abbey, Buckland, Buckfast, Tavistock, Hartland and Exeter's St Nicholas Priory all have evidence of the widespread destruction which followed.

1549 The people of the village of Sampford Courtenay start an uprising against the new prayer book almost by accident; an argument between the local peasants and gentry goes too far when one of the latter is killed. The peasants mass a small army and march on Exeter, with Cornish support. Thy are defeated and hundreds are executed.

1558 onwards The Age of the Navigators; Hawkins, Drake, Frobisher, Grenville and Gilbert were all Devon men. Drake set off to circumnavigate the world in 1577. During this era – where exploration often involved piracy – many forts were built along the south coast to protect the returning plunderers from their pursuers. Devon's farmers were kept busy supplying sailors and provisioning ships.

1588 Defeat of Spanish Armada, including Drake's famous moment of sangfroid, playing bowls on the Plymouth Hoe (in fact the tide was against his ships, and it would have been well-nigh impossible to leave harbour). Some captives of the Armada are incarcerated in the Spanish Barn at Torre Abbey, Torquay.

1620 The Pilgrim Fathers set sail from Plymouth in the *Mayflower* for America.

1642–46 Civil War. Exeter and Plymouth besieged by Royalists. Several skirmishes throughout the county. Fortified houses such as those at Bickleigh and Tiverton fall to the parliamentarians, and are considerably reduced in scale. Great Torrington captured by General Fairfax in 1646. Oliver Cromwell visits the county. Charles I is executed, and the future Charles II flees through Devon to safety on the Scilly Isles.

1649–60 The Commonwealth. Puritan rule, followed by the return of Charles II. One of his actions is to build the hugely powerful Citadel in Plymouth in 1666 – with some of its guns facing over the city, to repress any future uprising.

1688 William of Orange (William III) comes ashore in Brixham, and chooses Newton Abbot to declare his intentions to oust James II, before marching on London.

1769 Captain Cook makes his first voyage to Australia.

1790s Tin and copper mining bring prosperity to the region, with copper in particular peaking during the 1840s.

1806 Dartmoor prison built; only six years later it stood empty, following the introduction of deportation for convicts.

1815 Napoleon comes to South Devon as a prisoner on board the *Bellerophon*, on his way to exile in St Helena. Although he doesn't set foot on land, he proves quite a tourist attraction in both Plymouth harbour and Tor Bay.

1840s Isambard Kingdom Brunel brings the Great Western Railway to the West Country. Tourism, particularly beach tourism, develops rapidly as a result. Also during the 19th century substantial areas of industry move to the coal-rich areas of the Midlands and North. However, waterwheel-based industries persist in Devon, until even as recently at 1960 at Finch Foundry, near Okehampton.

1850s The practise of 'letterboxing' (*see page 69*) is first introduced on Dartmoor. It is revived in the 1970s, and is now very popular.

1872 The railway reaches North Devon.

1941 German air raids flatten the city of Plymouth and partially destroy Exeter.

1951 Dartmoor designated a National Park. Exmoor follows suit in 1954.

1952 24 hours of continuous rain cause the East and West Lyn rivers to flood massively, sweeping away much of Lynmouth and tragically killing 34 people.

1960s–80s The popularisation of the motor car prompts widespread transport and communications changes throughout the county, with the withdrawal of many rail links particularly to the north, the opening of the M5 motorway to Exeter, and the link road which acts as a motorway spur from Tiverton into North Devon. Joining the European Community has a negative impact on Devon's farmers, but produces inward funding for the development of rural areas.

1989 The Tarka Project is launched, designating much of Mid and North Devon as 'Tarka Country', setting up the 180-mile (288-km) Tarka Trail, and creating a local association whose members all adhere to a green charter.

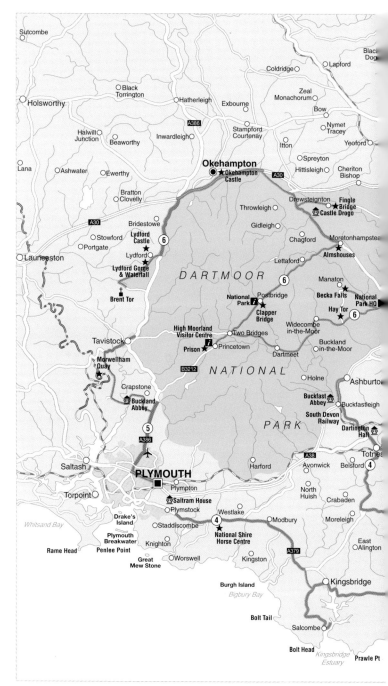

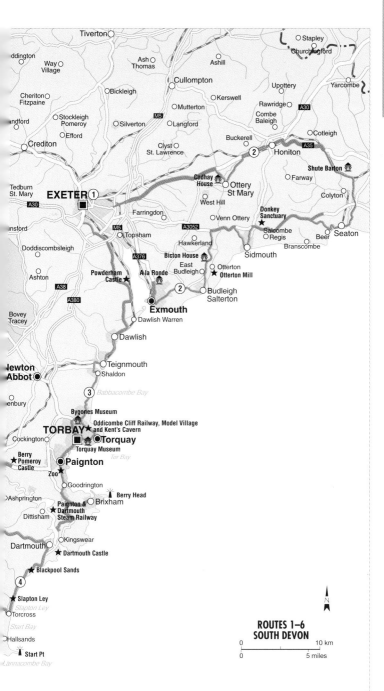

**ROUTES 1–6
SOUTH DEVON**

0   10 km

0   5 miles

Route 1

Exeter and Topsham

Cathedral – Underground Passages – St Nicholas Priory – Quayside – Maritime Museum – Topsham

The first recorded settlement (80–85BC) on the hilltop now occupied by **Exeter** was named Isca Dumnoniorum, after

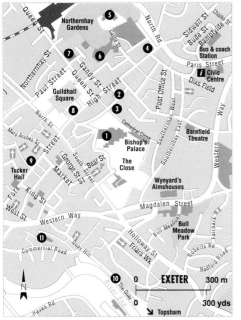

the local Dumnoniorum tribe who lived here. Not much more than 100 years later the Romans transferred their West Country base from Seaton to Exeter, and the city began to take shape. The city wall was completed in 200AD. Much of that wall is still standing and most of Exeter's key sights are within its circumference. The original Roman city lies underneath the modern pavements; in particular a bath house was discovered just opposite the cathedral, but had to be re-interred because of lack of funds.

In medieval times the city prospered through farming and the wool trade, and it hallmarked its own silver until the early 19th century. Its growth as a trading centre was hampered, however, by its position on the River Exe. As ships grew larger, the river's facilities became inadequate.

Today it is a bustling city (pop. 91,000) which administers the county of Devon. Students from its campus university prevent it from seeming too genteel.

The focal point for any visitor is the elegant **Cathedral Close**, screened from the modern city by a facade of buildings from a wide spread of styles and centuries.

At its centre, the ★★★ **Cathedral Church of St Peter** ❶ is largely 14th century, although its two Norman towers date from 1050, when Bishop Leofric first transferred his see to Exeter. The nave is of Beer stone, and was started by Bishop Bronescombe (1257–80) and then completed by Bishop Grandisson (1327–69).

Cathedral carvings

The visitor entrance is in the **West Front**, which is covered by figures of apostles and prophets (at ground level much weathered by inquisitive fingers). Inside, the most significant feature is the **fan vaulting**, which extends in a web of stone for 300ft (90m), the longest Gothic vault in the world. The eye is interrupted, however, by the carved **Quire screen**, illustrated with Biblical scenes and with the wooden organ (1665) perched on top. Along the left wall of the **nave** are embroidered bench-cushions known as the rondels, which tell the story of Exeter. In the north tower is the fully operational astronomical clock (1484).

Half way into the Quire stands the oak-carved **Bishop's Throne** (1312), like a medieval rocket. St James's Chapel, just behind it, replaces the only part of the building to be destroyed in World War II. At the far end is the delicately carved **Lady Chapel**, where the earliest bishops were buried and most of today's services are conducted.

The most eyecatching building in the close is the timber-framed 16th-century **Mol's Coffee House** ❷ (now

Mol's Coffee House

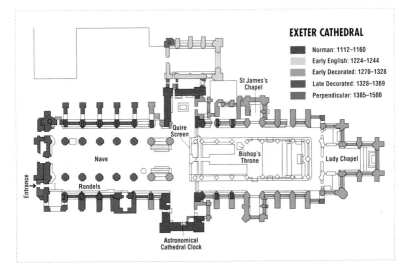

EXETER CATHEDRAL

- Norman: 1112–1160
- Early English: 1224–1244
- Early Decorated: 1270–1328
- Late Decorated: 1328–1369
- Perpendicular: 1385–1500

St James's Chapel

Quire Screen

Nave

Bishop's Throne

Lady Chapel

Entrance

Rondels

Astronomical Cathedral Clock

a jeweller's) where Sir Francis Drake supposedly met his captains. Diagonally across from Mol's is **The Royal Clarence**, founded in 1769, which claims the title of Britain's first hotel – although it was actually just the first to be called hotel, thanks to its French owner. Outside the Clarence is the meeting point for Exeter Council's free guided tours, which start at 11am (The Cathedral Close) and 2pm (Exeter Old and New).

Tacked onto the corner next to Mol's is the small sandstone **St Martin's church** ❸ (founded 1065) which has a slightly crooked interior. Up St Martin's Lane to the left is the Ship Inn, also a Drake hangout.

St Martin's Lane emerges onto the largely pedestrianised High Street. The post-war rebuilding of Exeter is clearly visible here: to the northeast the street widens into a vista of rather stolid modernism, while to the southwest it narrows into the uneven styles of old Exeter, still with some medieval wood-timbered frontages.

Beneath the pavements of the modern part are the **Underground Passages** ❹ (entrance in arcaded Roman Gate Passage), 14th-century tunnels which were carved out of the rock on the initiative of the clergy to help distribute water from a distant spring through the growing city. Although there is not much to see, the underground guided tours are entertaining and the experience unique, if cramped. (October to June, Tuesday to Friday 2–4.45pm, Saturday 10am–4.45pm; July to September, Monday to Saturday 10am–4.45pm).

County Court

Up the hill behind the passages is the former site of Rougemount Castle (so-called because of the red stone), now occupied by the Georgian **County Court** buildings ❺ (1774) and surrounded by gardens from where there is a good view over the city. On the other side of the High Street roads lead down to Southernhay, Exeter's financial district, with impressive Georgian terraces.

Inspired mural in Gandy Street

Retracing one's steps to St Martin's Lane, diagonally across to the south is the narrow **Gandy St**, with murals and speciality shops. At its end, topping a rise on the right, is the **Exeter & Devon Arts Centre** ❻, with a popular café and a heavy schedule of events.

Straight ahead is the ★ **Royal Albert Memorial Museum** ❼ (Monday to Saturday, 10am–5pm) a grand Victorian edifice with its entrance on Queen St. The Museum is strong on Devon's prehistory and Roman Exeter (including exhibits from the Roman bath house mentioned above). Its extensive natural history collection includes a tiger shot by King George V.

Back further down the High Street, on the right-hand side heading south, is the tottery-looking tudor portico of the **Guildhall** ❽. There has been a hall here from 1160, although the present building dates from the 14th century. It is the oldest functioning guildhall in the country, and while it is generally open during working hours, it closes during council meetings (tel: 01392-265500 to confirm).

As it starts to descend towards the river, High Street changes into Fore Street. Up a narrow right turn called Mint Lane is ★ **St Nicholas Priory** ❾ (Easter to October, Monday to Saturday 1–5pm), which is actually just the entertainment and accommodation block of the original 1087 priory; the rest was demolished by Henry VIII. The building has had many uses – private house, warehouse, mint – since its construction, but the kitchen and the Guest Hall are still impressively medieval. Previous residents include Martha the Raven, now in a glass case.

Returning to Fore St and descending the hill the other side of it, you will eventually reach the river Exe and the cobbled ★★ **Quayside** ❿ where history and nightlife live side by side. The old **Customs House** ⓫ (1681) is still in use, but the brick warehouses have been converted to shop and office accommodation. A visitor centre gives an impression of what Exeter's port was like during its heyday. In the 1560s a canal was built on the far side of the river, but that too failed to entice shipping up from Topsham (*see below*).

View over the quays

19

From the Customs House the line of the old city wall runs east to the site of South Gate and west to St Mary Steps church in West Street, where you will also find some fine 16th-century houses.

Sadly water transport is not available to ★★ **Topsham**, the estuary port at the mouth of the canal, 4 miles (6km) southeast of Exeter. During the height of the woollen trade in the 17th century, when the Exeter quayside began to prove inadequate, the merchants started to build grand houses on the shore at Topsham, creating an elegant waterside. Passenger steamers used to dock here until the railways came. The boatyards are still active.

Topsham was little touched by bombs, and its narrow-streeted charm is considerable – although it makes life difficult for motor vehicles. Antique shops, old inns, and restaurants line the main street, and along the Strand many of the houses are gable-ended, in imitation of Dutch style, a fashion introduced by Topsham merchants returning from Holland. All the houses have lovely views over the Exe estuary, a rich habitat for waterfowl. Among them is the Shell House (1718), named for the lovely scallop shell in its doorway.

Also on the Strand a small seasonal Museum (Monday, Wednesday, and Saturday, 2–5pm) tells the story of the rise and rise of this stylish port-resort, with special emphasis on its ship-building heyday.

Topsham town house

Route 2

East Devon

Exmouth – Sidmouth – Branscombe – Beer –Seaton-Honiton – Ottery St Mary *See map, p14–15*

East Devon has been largely ignored by mass tourism, and although as a region it contains few major sights, there's plenty to discover amongst the folds of its quiet hills. Inland it is farming country dotted by market towns and country houses, while on the coast gently elegant seaside resorts crowd down steep valleys.

Finding shelter in Exmouth

This tour begins at **Exmouth**, where the Exe estuary meets the sea. Exmouth's 2 miles (3km) of golden sand are the finest in East Devon, and were the key to it becoming Devon's first beach resort back in the 18th century. The neat town centre square belies the way the town sprawls, and its population of 30,000 puts it third in Devon (excluding the tourist region of Torbay). The sea front Esplanade has all the traditional attractions of a beach holiday, as well as an important windsurfing centre.

A La Ronde

Two miles out of Exmouth just off the Exeter road is ★ **A La Ronde** (April to October, Sunday to Thursday, 11am–5.30pm; National Trust) high on the hill with tremendous views out over the estuary. This eccentric 16-sided house was designed in 1795 by Jane Parminter, who, helped by her cousin Mary, decorated it with feathers and seashells, seaweed and sand, cut paper and marbled paint. The Shell Gallery in particular is a tour de force. The Parminters set up their own charity, Point in View, designed to benefit elderly spinsters and to encourage Jewish women to adopt Christianity.

Budleigh Salterton

Leaving Exmouth, the A376 winds around the hills before descending into **Budleigh Salterton**. Sir Walter Raleigh, who was born a couple of miles away at East Budleigh, was depicted on the beach here in a painting by Sir John Millais, *The Boyhood of Raleigh*. Budleigh has a long shingle beach within its red-cliff framed bay, backed at the east end by salt flats where the river Otter exits to the sea (thus 'Salterton'). The core of the town fights shy of the sea-front, clinging to the long main street as it winds up the hill. It is a retiring, genteel sort of place.

Two miles (3km) inland, in the direction of Bicton, is a crossroads with a brick signpost which dates from 1743. Right here is the village of **Otterton**, lined with attractive whitewashed cob houses and with a small stream running down alongside the main street to meet the river Otter. In 1414 there were two woollen mills and a flour mill in the village, and – hard to believe today – seafaring boats

could anchor beside the bridge. The woollen mills have gone, but the ★ **flour mill** is still there, in a complex which includes a restaurant, craft shop, bakery and museum.

A couple of miles further up the road are **Bicton Park** and **Bicton House**. Henry Rolle's original country house garden design of 1730 has been embellished with themed areas, palm house, museum and a woodland railway.

Baking bread at Otterton
On a pedestal, Bicton Park

A right turn on the A3052 will bring you down into the crowded valley of **Sidmouth**, the most attractive and best preserved of East Devon's resorts. Narrow lanes of tearooms and traditional shops back onto a grand seafront dominated by a parade of Regency houses with wrought-iron balconies. The beach, framed by 500-ft (150-m) cliffs on either side, is largely shingle, although there is some sand at low tide. Queen Victoria spent a winter here when she was a little girl.

In the 17th century Sidmouth was just a fishing village, and a handful of fishing boats still operate from the east end of the beach. The other end is host to a fine cricket pitch, in what must be one of the finest locations in the country. Sidmouth has elegant small hotels and a couple of museums, but its main cultural attraction is the International Festival of Folk Song and Dance, during the first week in August, when these very English lanes are filled with very un-English sights and sounds.

21

The A3052 continues east. A couple of miles out of Sidmouth, down a narrow lane to the right, is the ★ **Donkey Sanctuary** (daily, 9am–dusk), a rest home for abused donkeys, which incorporates some nine farms and 160 staff. The sanctuary is a tribute to the single-mindedness of one woman, Dr Elizabeth Svendsen, and has taken some 6,600 beasts into its care.

From the sanctuary a narrow lane leads down into

Donkeys ahead
A corner of Sidmouth

Misty day in Branscombe

Below Beer

22

Pullman at the Pecorama

★★ **Branscombe**, (meaning branched combe or valley). There are corners of real beauty and character here; at the top end of the village is the 12th-century Norman church dedicated to the Welsh saint St Winifred. Grapes used to be grown in this sheltered valley for the monks of Sherborne Abbey.

Further down the road passes an active, thatched smithy, and then forks right down towards the beach. The latter is very undeveloped: the Tea Shanty tearoom occupies pride of place, while a row of coastguard cottages just up the hill have been turned into a hotel. Such heavy coastguard presence testifies to days when smuggling was prevalent, and up in the Branscombe graveyard is the tomb of a coastguard officer who died in the line of duty.

Branscombe was also known for its lace-makers, as was the next-door village of **Beer** (derived from 'beare', meaning wood), up over the hill. But besides smuggling and lace, Beer's fame comes also from its limestone, used to build Exeter cathedral and many other great churches and country houses of the region. Beer stone is unusual in that it is relatively soft and easy to quarry, but hardens on exposure to air. Part of the former underground workings are open to the public, on the Branscombe to Beer road, in ★ **Beer Quarry Caves** (daily, April to September, 10am–5pm). In these vaulted caverns everything was done by hand; many of the masons carved their names on the walls, and the pick marks made by the Romans are still visible.

Up the hill above Beer is the **Pecorama** (indoor exhibition all year, outdoor attractions April to September, 10am–5pm), essentially a well-landscaped paradise for miniature railway enthusiasts sited next to the Peco factory which specialises in such railways.

The village of Beer itself clusters around a short main street which ends with a short drop to the beach, covered in fishing boats which are winched up and down the shingle. Beer's buccaneering past is still remembered in an annual regatta.

It is difficult to tell where Beer ends and **Seaton** begins, but the two places are very different. Seaton is a big, holiday-camp based resort spread across the flat of the Axe valley, with little interest other than the **Electric Tramway**, which runs in summer months up the valley to the small town of Colyton.

The journey is worth making, not just for the tram ride: **Colyton** itself has much charm, and an unusual history. Colyton has its own councillors, or Feoffes, originally 20 merchants who bought the parish from Henry VIII for £1,000, and it has changed little since then. Feoffes still run the administrative affairs of Colyton, putting their resources to 'good, godly and commendable purposes'.

The church of St Andrews is topped by an unusual lantern which was added in the 15th century, supposedly to provide a beacon for ships sailing up the Axe valley.

On the side of the Shute road out of Colyton stands the imposing gateway of **Shute Barton** (April to October, Wednesday and Saturday 2–5.30pm), started in 1380. The Pole family bought the house in 1560. Their descendants still live here, giving the guided tour added interest.

Shute Barton

Continue on through the country lanes to the market town of **Honiton**, administrative capital of East Devon. Honiton's Georgian architecture and unhurried broad street is the product of devastating fires in the 17th–18th centuries, although the town dates back to the 12th century. As recently as 1852 there were 4,101 makers of Honiton lace in the area, but the industry has since died. Presentation pieces are still made privately, and have been worn by all the recent royal babies. Fine examples are kept in Allhallows museum and Honiton Lace Shop, both in the town centre. The strange Hot Pennies Ceremony persists in the annual fair in July, when heated pennies are thrown amongst the children.

A third of the way back to Exeter, south of the A30, is **Ottery St Mary**, a particularly attractive largely 17th- and 18th-century town (Otrei in the Domesday book) wedged into a small valley. Coleridge was born here.

Up a steep hill from the centre is the church of ★★ **St Mary**, a stunning replica of Exeter cathedral, far more impressive from the inside than out. The church was founded by Bishop Grandisson, who completed Exeter cathedral, and has a 14th-century astronomical clock, just like Exeter, although where the cathedral has fan vaulting St Mary's has pencil and rib. Tradition has it that every year wicked pixies try to abduct the bellringers. The other strange Ottery tradition is the annual Barrel Ritual (5 November) when tar-soaked barrels are lit and carried blazing through the crowds on the shoulders of local men.

On the west side of the town is an odd, circular tumbling weir like a giant plughole, created in 1791 to power a serge factory (now making electrical components).

A mile or so northwest of Ottery, and visible from the B3176, is ★ **Cadhay** (July, August, Wednesday to Friday, 2–6pm, or parties by appointment, tel: 01404-812432), a private house built around 1550 by solicitor John Haydon, probably using stone from local churches demolished by Henry VIII. There are many different hands at work within, and every room has a different character. It is the residence of the William-Powletts, indirect descendants of John Haydon, one of whom may even be your guide.

From Cadhay it is a mile to the A30, and thence back to Exeter.

23

Customers welcome

Route 3

The English Riviera

Powderham Castle – Dawlish – Teignmouth – Torquay – Babbacombe – Paignton *See map, p14–15*

From Dawlish to the river Dart, Devon dedicates itself to tourism. This southeast-facing coast is sheltered from the prevailing winds, and is thus a few degrees warmer, winter and summer, making resorts out of fishing villages. The main attraction here is Torbay – an administrative combination of Torquay, Paignton and Brixham with a population of 127,000 and 22 miles (35km) of coastline within the great sweep of Tor Bay. This 'English Riviera' attracts 1.5 million visitors a year.

However, anyone setting off from Exeter would be foolish to miss a few sights on the way.

A short drive southwest, in a stunning location in parkland overlooking the estuary, is ★★ **Powderham Castle** (daily, April to October, 10am–5.30pm) which has always been home to the Courtenay family, earls of Devon, and featured in the film *Remains of the Day*. The building dates from 1390, although it has notable later additions. The interior is grand and dramatic, and efforts have been made to make the guided tours entertaining. A favourite is the oldest resident – 150-year-old Timothy the tortoise. Organised tractor and trailer rides go through the deer park.

Powderham's main entrance originally faced the estuary, but then Brunel bought the foreshore from the Courtenays and the Crown and built his railway. Today the line is a feature of this shoreline for many miles, and at the resort of **Dawlish** it frames the sea and the town. Dawlish first became popular towards the end of the 18th century, and both Charles Dickens and Jane Austen stayed here. Today it is a place of no great pretension, which gets most of its character from the Long Lawn which runs down to the beach, and the Bubbling Brook at its centre, which is home to black swans. Wilder bird life can be found on **Dawlish Warren**, the sandbar that covers most of the entrance to the Exe estuary, and which is also a popular picnic site on sunny days.

Teignmouth, further down the A379, has a split personality. To the open sea it presents itself as a resort, complete with Grand Pier (built in the 1860s) and long beach, while the other cheek of the town lies along the estuary of the river Teign and is still a working port. Both aspects have seen better days. In the narrow streets between is the town centre and pedestrian shopping areas, while up the hill just the other side of the ring road is the church of **St James the Less**, with an unusual lantern tower.

Pleasures of the pier

The coast road crosses the Teign estuary via a former toll bridge to the pretty village of **Shaldon**, and then climbs the hill behind it, affording good views of the estuary.

You are now entering the Torbay area, although this approach is rather uninspiring. It is not until the ★★ **sea-front** that the best side of **Torquay** is revealed. The town is formed around inner and outer harbours, filled with leisure boating, a pier and spacious esplanade. The main shopping street, pedestrianised and with modern arcades, tunnels back up the valley. The harbourside and seafront promenade boasts cafés, boat trips (particularly to Brixham and up the river Dart), theatres and the **Pavilion**, a lovely example of Edwardian cream-cake sea-side architecture, once a theatre but now filled with shops.

Could almost be Cannes

Torquay emphasises its Mediterranean influences, and at night when the illuminations are on, the palm trees rustling, and the people promenading, it could almost be Cannes or Monte Carlo.

Home from home in Torquay

Several main attractions concentrate around the former village of **Babbacombe**, on the north side of the Torquay promontory. The focus here is manicured lawns on the top of an east-facing cliff overlooked by elegant small hotels, with Oddicombe beach way down below. The beach is reached by a zigzagging road, or by the ★ **Oddicombe Cliff Railway** (April to October), an attraction in itself. A short walk inland from the cliffs is the ★★ **Babbacombe Model Village** (daily, Easter to September, 9am–10pm, October to Easter, 9am–dusk), a microcosm of contemporary England, complete with sound and movement, done with considerable care and humour (look for the Ann Teak furniture shop and Penny Sillin the chemist). The village was started in 1963, but has evolved continuously and is particularly fine at dusk, when the lights go on.

Peering out to sea

A short walk away, in Fore St, is ★★ **Bygones** (daily, March to October 10am–6pm, November to February, an indoor fantasyland, with a recreated Victorian shopping street, model railways galore, fantasy world scenes (created by a former prisoner of war) and a rather odd World War I trench experience.

A couple of miles east along the same road is ★★ **Kent's Cavern** (daily, 10am–5pm, with late opening in summer), a network of limestone caves created two million years ago by underground rivers. The enlarging caves served as water filters and lairs for predatory animals, and more than 80,000 archaeological artefacts have been found here, including 18,000-year-old mammoth bones. A massive cave bear is fossilised into the roof of one chamber. The discoveries made in these caves rewrote history, particularly that of the oldest human remains in Europe, a 31,000-year-old jaw of a teenager. The guided tour is good, and you may have the opportunity to handle a bit of fossilised hyena dung, but many of the best remains are now housed in **Torquay museum** (Monday to Saturday, 10am–4.45pm), at the foot of Babbacombe Road.

On the other side of the harbour, standing a little back from the seafront in its own grounds, is Torquay's historic ★ **Torre Abbey** (Easter to October, 9.30am–6pm), which despite its name is mainly an art gallery, with abbey ruins attached. Only the gatehouse and the tithe barn outside (known as the Spanish barn because it once housed captured sailors from the Spanish armada) pre-date the abbey's destruction; the gatehouse is 14th-century, while the barn dates from the founding of the abbey in 1196. The main building was built up as a private house during the 18th century.

Also here is an Agatha Christie room, containing mementos of Torquay's most celebrated daughter, who visited the abbey socially when it was still a private house.

Beyond Torre lies **Cockington**, a preserved rural village and country house in grounds that reach almost to the sea. There are many more remarkable villages in Devon, but this one's position makes it worth a visit.

In the centre of Tor Bay Torquay blends seamlessly into **Paignton**, which sprawls over flatter land. Paignton has little of the elegance of Torquay but it does have the advantage of two of the region's best stretches of sand, off the promenade in front of the town centre and at Goodrington, a couple of miles further on. Goodrington can be reached on the ★ **Paignton & Dartmouth Steam Railway** (April to October), which sets off from Paignton and chugs through attractive coastal scenery to its terminus at Kingswear, on the Dart estuary, from where boat tours are available.

Cockington carriage ride
Postcard image

Up the valley behind Goodrington is the ★ **Paignton Zoo** (daily 10am–6pm), well-landscaped and innovative, and home to over 50 endangered species. Micro-environments recreated here include Devon woodland, savannah and tropical rainforest.

Brixham harbour

27

Beyond Paignton the bay becomes less populated, and the road winds through countryside before descending to the small resort of **Brixham**, where tourism sits alongside a flourishing fishing fleet. The ★★ **harbour area** of Brixham has real character, both as a working and leisure port with extensive marina, and in the early morning has a very active fish market (not open to the public).

Moored in the inner harbour is a replica of the *Golden Hind*, the ship that took Devonian Francis Drake around the world. On the quay is a statue of William of Orange, marking where he came ashore in 1688 to claim the English throne.

The coastal road leads up onto the last headland in Tor Bay. Grassy ★ **Berry Head** has been turned into a country park, and it too has historical landmarks: the remains of two forts built in 1803 during the Napoleonic Wars. It's a breezy place where locals walk their dogs, and its sheer 200-ft (60-m) limestone cliffs are home to guillemots, known locally as Brixham penguins.

Berry Head

The northern fort is better preserved and commands a better view (its guardroom is now a tearoom), but the forts' 1,000 soldiers didn't see much action. When Napoleon did make it into the broad sweep of the bay he was a prisoner, on his way to exile in St Helena.

A short drive back and over the headland from here (the steam railway takes the most scenic route) is the town of **Kingswear**, clinging to the steep banks of the Dart estuary, and with the more appealing town of **Dartmouth** (*see Route 4, page 31*) opposite, a brief ferry ride away.

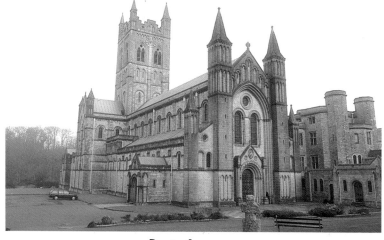

Buckfast Abbey

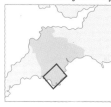

Route 4

The South Hams

Buckfastleigh – Totnes – Dartmouth – Salcombe
See map p14–15

The South Hams is a large, essentially rural area between the Dart and the Tamar, a flowing and verdant beard under the stony face of Dartmoor. The name derives from the old English 'hamme', meaning an enclosed and sheltered place. Down its mazy lanes lie nuggets of great interest and beauty, whose highlights include one of Devon's finest old towns (Totnes) and a historic and handsome port (Dartmouth). It has beaches and cliffs, forests and vineyards, deep river valleys and smugglers' coves.

This route begins just beyond the gateway town of Newton Abbot, where the imposing town of **Ashburton** stands just north of the A38. Ashburton is a Dartmoor gateway and one of four strategically-placed former stannary towns (with Plympton, Tavistock and Chagford) where tin from mines was weighed and appropriate duty paid. Its tall and well-preserved 17th- and 18th-century houses reflect the ensuing prosperity. A landmark is the old Golden Lion pub, which doubles as the headquarters of the Monster Raving Loony party.

Party headquarters

There used to be a regular agricultural market on the granite slabs in and around what is now the Town Hall on North Street, but Ashburton's shops today specialise in antique furniture and furnishings. The river Ashburn chases under and around the houses in its hurry to join the Dart; once it powered several woollen mills, and regularly flooded until prevention measures were taken higher up the valley.

The Dart broadens considerably as it heads south, brushing past the hidden town of **Buckfastleigh**. The latter had the woollen industry (five mills still operating in 1890) but missed out on the tin wealth of Ashburton, and as a result is on a smaller scale, with small courtyards leading off its narrow main street. The textile industry is still here at the Buckfast Mill (visitor centre) which spins yarn for Axminster carpets, a mile upstream from the town. The mill merges almost seamlessly into the complex of buildings that surrounds ★★ **Buckfast Abbey** (9am–5.30pm), excellently preserved, and clearly laid out with something other than commercial interest in mind.

The Abbey church

The amazing story of Buckfast is well told in a small exhibition in the original guest hall. The Abbey was founded by Cistercian monks in 1018, then destroyed in 1539 on the orders of Henry VIII; the roof was stripped and the weather did the rest. The ruin was bought in 1882 by a group of French Benedictine monks for £4,900, and they and their successors began the laborious task of rebuilding, with no prior experience or skills. It wasn't until 1936, with an average of four monks working over 30 years, that Buckfast was finished.

The Abbey church itself, Norman in style, has a certain freshness inside. And nowhere more so than behind the choir in the Chapel of the Blessed Sacrament (added in 1966), with its glass Christ with arms outstretched.

Buckfast's stained-glass Christ

There are 38 industrious monks at Buckfast. When they're not praying they're serving in the shops, beekeeping or making tonic wine and coloured glass. The abbey produce shop uphill from the car park carries a revealing cross-section of products from other self-supporting abbeys of Europe.

Between the town and abbey is the ★ **South Devon Railway** (April to October), also known as the Primrose Line, a steam-hauled service on former GWR tracks that follow the Dart to Totnes. There's a model railway and Butterfly Farm & Otter Sanctuary at Buckfastleigh station.

Travel on the train, however, and you miss the widely scattered **Dartington estate**, 2 miles (3km) north of Totnes. Most visited is the **Cider Press Centre**, a well-designed group of 12 shops housed in and around a former cider-making building. Much of the high-quality merchandise reflects the Dartington emphasis on arts and crafts, with a particularly good selection of local foods.

This is the commercial side of the Dartington Trust, the creation of wealthy philanthropists Leonard and Dorothy Elmhirst, he English and she American, who had in mind a regeneration of rural life when they bought the Hall in 1925. His interest was in agriculture and hers arts and crafts, but the trust is now widely influential county-wide

Dartington Hall gardens

in many guises – the Plough Arts Centre, Dartington Glass (*see page 48*), Morwellham Quay (*see page 37*) and even in Dartmoor prison, where the trust provides much-needed further education.

For the nerve centre, turn off the main road by Dartington church and follow it up a slow hill to the arts encampment over the brow, with gallery, college and research centres. Here ★★ **Dartington Hall** (built in the 14th century) has the atmosphere of an Oxbridge college, gathered around its cobbled quad, and with a magnificent hammer-beamed Great Hall. Visitors can walk through to view the hall and the gardens beyond, where a variety of sculptures and a grassy-banked amphitheatre are set in mature woodland.

The Dart becomes navigable at **Totnes**, a town of refinement frequently described as 'Elizabethan'. In fact its known history dates back to 959AD, when 'Totta's Ness' (fort on a ness or ridge of ground) was established as a walled town by the kingdom of Wessex. It became a centre for cloth trade, and in Henry VIII's time was the second richest town in Devon after Exeter. The port has only recently stopped receiving cargo. Despite its history, it is also arty and fashionably alternative.

The face of Totnes has not changed for centuries, stretching up its one main street towards where the castle is concealed from view by a tumble of crowding houses. At the river end of this street stands the memorial to William John Wills, a Totnesian who became the first man to cross Australia on foot (1861) and then foolishly tried to retrace his steps. Thereafter a variety of passages and frontages (Totnes' seasonal Elizabethan Museum is in a Tudor house at number 70) are interrupted by the arch of the East Gate across the road, marking the town wall. A steep right directly under the arch leads up onto the ramparts and round to the ★★ **Guildhall** (Easter to October, Monday to Friday, 10am–5pm), a lovely building behind a pillared portico (17th-century granite pillars moved from the main street in 1897) that has its origins in a Benedictine priory of 1088, although the current structure is largely 16th century. The monthly council meeting still gathers around the table where Cromwell sat in 1646, and the list of mayors dates back to 1359, except for a gap in the 14th century when plague ravaged the town.

The Guildhall was once a grammar school, and also served as the town jail and mortuary – very conveniently placed for the neighbouring **St Mary's Church** (15th-century) in local red sandstone, but with a delicate and slightly tottery Saxon rood screen carved from Beer stone.

The main street opens out into the Market Place, with the 17th-century granite pillared **Butterwalk** on one side

East Gate

and rather unfortunate 1960s civic architecture opposite. This is the venue on summer Tuesdays for the Elizabethan market, with traders in period dress.

Turn right at the end of the Butterwalk and within a hundred yards ★★ **Totnes Castle** (daily from 10am, April to October, and Wednesday to Sunday in winter) looms overhead. This is a plain, but perfectly preserved Norman motte and bailey structure, a circular crown on the roof of the town, whose simplicity adds to its power. One way the eye travels over crowded rooftops, and the other it climbs up onto Dartmoor.

Castle view and the Norman Keep

A short distance out of Totnes just off the Paignton road is **Berry Pomeroy Castle**, a romantic ruin that has the reputation of Devon's most haunted castle, with pleasant woodland walks.

The road from Totnes to Dartmouth is slow and windy, and there are plenty of potential diversions. Off to the left at Harberton is the vineyard of **Ashprington**, with walks and tastings, and not far away through the attractive hamlet of **Capton** is a prehistoric hill settlement – a reconstructed neolithic round house on the corner of a pick-your-own fruit field. A couple of narrow roads also lead down to the shore-side village of **Dittisham**, home to a few retired millionaires, with great views and a passenger ferry across the Dart. Not an easy place to bring a car.

31

Dartmouth itself is in a sheltered location on the west bank of the Dart estuary, facing the small town of Kingswear (two vehicle and one passenger ferry make the crossing through the year). The waters are thick with boats in one of Britain's best anchorages.

Dartmouth has a long maritime history, and a strong navy presence on its shores and back up the hill above the town, where the **Britannia Royal Naval College** puts would-be officers (including several in the Royal Family) through their paces.

★★★ **Downtown Dartmouth** focuses around what is called the **Boat Float** – an inner harbour full of dingies – and the streets that run off it, crowded with historic buildings with fine frontages covered in painted heads, coats of arms, and stained and leaded glass. A pleasant bandstand and garden (with palm trees testifying to the gentle climate) occupy one side of the Float, with the **tourist information office** in the same building as a small exhibition housing a working steam engine to commemorate Thomas Newcomen, inventor, who was born in Dartmouth in 1663.

Dartmouth's Boat Float

On the prom between the Float and the estuary stands the Station restaurant, Britain's only station without tracks: passengers would buy their train tickets here then hop on the ferry across to Kingswear, where the steam train from Paignton (*see page 26*) runs right down to the quay. The passenger ferry still runs, and if you don't take any other boat trip, then be sure to at least just nip over to Kingswear – whose main attraction is its view.

(*see page 26*)

On the other side of the Float, Duke St has its own granite-pillared 17th-century **Butterwalk** (small museum here), better preserved than the one at Totnes. Just up here,

Foss Street

past the crossroads with pedestrianised Foss Street, is the solid old market, built around a cobbled square in 1828. Much of this land has been reclaimed, which explains why the oldest houses and church are to be found not here but just up the hill off the top left corner of the Float.

St Saviour's (founded in 1286) has fine stained glass and a wood-panelled ceiling, a pulpit shaped like a chalice and a huge medieval iron door. Round the corner in Higher Street are Exchange Brasserie, a timber-framed frontage from 1352 built originally by the mayor, and a few doors along the **Cherub** (1380), a three-tiered pub with good food. Returning to quay level and heading away from the Float, it's a short walk to **Bayards Cove**, by the ferry landing. Bayards is less of a cove and more a well-preserved shore front, and it is no surprise to learn that films have been made here. At the end of the short prom is a walk-in artillery fort built by Dartmouth Corporation in 1510, where high tide laps right up to the gunholes.

32

Bigger fortifications are a mile or so further. **Dartmouth Castle** (daily, April to October, 10am–6pm, Wednesday to Sunday in winter, 10am–4pm) clamped to a shoulder of rock where the Dart meets the sea, is actually three elements: a Victorian artillery fort, the original castle (1481) and St Petrock's church (1642, although there's been a church here since the 12th century). The artillery fort is so strong it seems more like an underground chamber than a man-made structure. Dartmouth was invaded by a group of rampaging French in 1404, which prompted the first fortifications, but after the original fort was completed – and a chain could be stretched across to Kingswear castle on the opposite shore – the town was never invaded again.

Welcome aboard

The best way to see these castles and the Dart estuary – which is pretty inaccessible by road other than at Dartmouth – is on a ★★ **boat trip**. Hidden creeks, imposing private houses, birdlife and sloping vineyards line its navigable 12 miles (19km) to Totnes.

Blackpool Sands

Heading south from Dartmouth the cliffs drop away first to **Blackpool Sands**, a lovely golden curve of a beach, very undeveloped despite its name, and then to run along the broad shingle at **Slapton Ley**, where an inland freshwater lake is thick with birds. US forces trained here for the Normandy landings of 1944, and locals had to leave their houses. Sadly, disaster struck in the shape of a sub-

View of Start Point

marine attack during training, and 946 soldiers were killed. The tank in the car park at **Torcross** was recovered from the seabed, and serves as memorial.

The road dives inland here, but there is a fine cliff walk to **Start Point**, via the remains of a village that has crumbled into the sea at Hallsands.

33

Kingsbridge and Salcombe, respectively at the head and mouth of a 5-mile (8-km) sea inlet, mirror Totnes and Dartmouth, although on a more minor scale. **Kingsbridge**'s steep main street is reminiscent of Totnes, as are its passages (find the aptly-named Squeezebelly Lane just to the left of the Heritage Inn). Its town hall (incorporating theatre and cinema) has a clock with three faces: the fourth side is blank, because it once faced the workhouse. At the top of the hill is a 16th-entury granite-pillared Shambles, once a row of butcher's stalls but now a tearoom.

★ **Salcombe**'s sailing clippers used to bring back the first fruit harvest from the Caribbean, so it's appropriate that this fishing village has become a big yachting centre thronged with people on the weekend. Sandy bays on the other side of the inlet are a short ferry ride from the town quay.

Cool couple in Salcombe

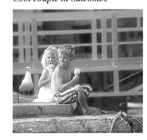

The coastline westwards from here is one of shipwrecks and secret smuggler's coves. Inland, too, is a hidden rural landscape that repays exploration.

Beyond the handsome 18th-century town of **Modbury**, en route to Plymouth, is one further family-orientated attraction: the **National Shire Horse Centre** (daily 10am–5pm, November to March 10am–4pm) at Yealmpton. Besides the 40-odd shires, which include King, the world's tallest horse, the centre has a wide variety of animals and small exhibitions, and stages falconry shows and shire parades through the day.

From here it is a short drive to Plymouth.

Seaside and poolside

Route 5

West Devon

Plymouth – Buckland Abbey – Morwellham – Tavistock *See map p14–15*

The largest conurbation in Devon, **Plymouth** (population 250,000) was once three townships: Dock (now Devonport), Sutton and Stonehouse. Although it is only a few miles from the downtown stores to the bleak uplands of Dartmoor, the contrast couldn't be greater.

The natural harbour formed where the rivers Tamar and Plym debouch into the Sound was already a significant port in the 14th century, and an obvious choice for a naval base to control the western end of the Channel. Numerous discoverers and pioneers set off on their epic voyages from here: Drake, Hawkins, Raleigh, Cook, the Pilgrim Fathers and half a million emigrants. Significantly, there are 40 other Plymouths dotted around the world. In fact, such was the port's success that in the 19th century Dock was the largest town in Devon. It later petitioned to change its name to Devonport.

But being a naval base also made the city a target at times of war; in one night in 1941, 1,000 people were killed and 20,000 homes destroyed by German bombs. When the war ended, town planners scrapped what remained and started again. The result is pragmatic pedestrian shopping on a massive traffic island.

Fortunately, the setting for many of Plymouth's best dramas is still in place: the ★★ **Hoe** ⑫ (old English for 'high place') is a broad grassy shoulder between town and sea, and it commands a tremendous view of the Sound, laid out below like an amphitheatre. Nuclear submarines may slip around the world unnoticed, but there's no avoiding the viewers on the Hoe. This is where Sir Francis Drake was playing bowls at the sighting of the Spanish Armada.

At hand is Drake's Island, Plymouth's own Alcatraz, which was fortified by Drake and at one time used as a prison (until Princetown on Dartmoor was completed). In the middle distance is the long low line of the Breakwater (29 years to build, completed in 1840) which gave Plymouth the largest and safest harbour in Britain. A derelict fortress sits just beside it. In the far distance (14 miles/23km) the Eddystone lighthouse can be seen on a clear day. The current lighthouse is the fourth; the third – **Smeaton's Tower ⓭** – stands on the Hoe, and is open to the public. It was moved here in 1884, after 123 years on the rocks, because its foundations had begun to erode.

A selection of memorials lines the Hoe towards the formidable walls of the ★ **Royal Citadel ⓮** (guided tours in summer, at 12 noon and 2pm). The fort was completed in 1671 by Charles II, shortly after Plymouth had taken the anti-royalist side in the Civil War, and its guns face both ways – over the city and the sea – although they have never been fired in anger. The Citadel is garrisoned by the Royal Artillery.

Well landscaped into the front brow of the Hoe is the ★★ **Dome ⓯** (open daily from 9am), an innovative multimedia presentation of Plymouth's past and present, which brings history to life, and provides hands-on experience of modern navigation equipment.

Hotels on the Hoe

Smeaton's Tower

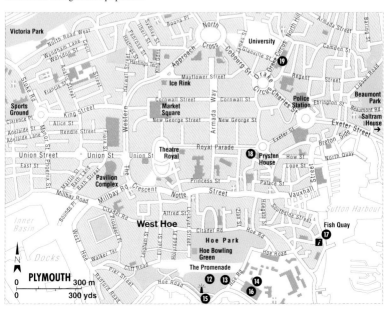

Turning left out of the Dome, the road curls around underneath the Citadel below the **Aquarium** ⑯, a small collection of tanks attached to an important marine research centre. A big project is under way to open a grand new National Marine Aquarium at a site round the corner in Sutton Harbour in 1998.

The Barbican

Sutton Harbour is the watery part of the ★★ **Barbican** ⑰, a preserved corner of Plymouth as it used to be, from where many of Plymouth's historic voyages started out. Today Sutton is for fishing and leisure boats, with a large fishmarket on the far quay. Naval and commercial harbours are found round in the Tamar estuary on the other side of the Hoe, and can best be seen by boat trip from the Barbican quayside.

The Barbican's shops, restaurants and galleries are attractively located in converted warehouses and merchants' houses, particularly along Southside Street. The Warehouse that Jack Built boasts a tall mural by local artist Robert Lenkiewizc; walk through the arcade of eccentric shops within and you'll emerge near another, larger Lenkiewizc. Towards the end of the street is the **Plymouth gin distillery**, which welcomes visitors, although part of the building has been attractively converted to a pub and restaurant with stills etc in situ.

Lenkiewizc mural

36

Plymouth is a city without a cathedral. Its **St Andrew's church** ⑱ was largely rebuilt following the war, and is notable for some very striking glass windows by artist John Piper, as well as graffiti scratched into the masonry which is thought to date from the Drake era and to celebrate the latter's voyage round the world.

The **City Museum and Art Gallery** ⑲ (Tuesday to Friday, 10am–5.30pm), behind the main shopping area, reflects local interests in a generalised collection, but also has fine paintings by Burne-Jones and Stanhope Forbes.

Saltram House

In Plymouth's eastern suburbs stands the grand ★★ **Saltram House** (April to October, Sunday to Thursday, 12.30–5.30pm; National Trust), Devon's largest country house, in 470 acres (190ha) of grounds and 13 acres (5.3ha) of gardens. The house dates from the late 16th century, and most of the work on it was done by the landowning Parker family. It is unique in that virtually all its furnishings are original, including a huge quantity of paintings, many by Sir Joshua Reynolds who was a friend of the Parker family.

In the 1770s Robert Adam reworked some rooms, including the magnificent saloon, where the pattern on the carpet mirrors the plasterwork on the ceiling. The showrooms are only a fraction of the whole. Saltram House served as the Dashwood family home in the film of *Sense and Sensibility*.

Due north of the city on the way to Tavistock are two high-lights of West Devon. ★ **Buckland Abbey** (daily except Thursday, April to October, 10.30am–5.30pm; Saturday and Sunday 2–5pm in winter; National Trust) dates from 1278, although it only spent 259 years as a Cistercian abbey before the dissolution. Its original outlines have been disguised in the course of succeeding centuries, but the original abbey church is still its heart, albeit adapted and converted. The Cistercians were farmers, and their vast oak-roofed barn, which remains much as it was when it was built in the early 1300s, is evidence of the substantial scale of their lands and crops.

Buckland Abbey

Buckland's most famous era, however, was as the home of Drake (born in nearby Tavistock), who bought the house in 1580 from his rival Sir Richard Grenville for £3,400, a fortune at the time. Sadly much of the building was gutted by fire but the plaster, carving and panelling of the Tudor Great Room escaped, as did Drake's Drum. The rooms house an exhibition devoted to Drake.

A handful of miles north is ★★★ **Morwellham Quay** (daily, 10am–5.30pm), the highest navigable point on the Tamar. Morwellham is a superbly preserved and presented snapshot of how industry and thus transport ebbed and flowed in the region in Victorian times. It is set in a lovely valley, and animated by staff in period costume.

Morwellham mill and canal

Morwellham existed as a port for a thousand years before the discovery of huge copper deposits in the region demanded the provision of heavy transport – so much so that a canal was cut from Tavistock to the hills above Morwellham, from where an inclined railway ran down to the quay. Morwellham also has its own copper mine, and a small railway takes interested visitors a quarter of a mile into the hill.

Eventually the mines were exhausted and the railway arrived, killing off water transport. Morwellham disappeared under weeds until 1970, when it became a project of the Dartington Trust *(see page 29)*, which lovingly restored and created its museums and trails.

Tavistock benefited enormously from the prosperity of local copper and tin mining. The landowning Russell family (dukes of Bedford) created the town as it looks today, particularly the main Bedford Square, with its greenish-stoned Victorian town hall and guildhall dominating one side. This whole area was the site of an abbey originally founded in 974, of which only a few scattered remnants are still extant. Plunge through the arch near the tourist office and you will reach the town's active and characterful pannier market.

Tavistock is only 10 miles (16km) from Plymouth, but it belongs to another world altogether.

Route 6

Dartmoor

Bovey Tracey – Widcombe-in-the-Moor – Prince-town – Chagford – Okehampton *See map, p14–15*

The Dartmoor National Park covers some 365 sq. miles (945 sq. km) of south-central Devon. Although the moor is governed by the park authority, the land is still largely in private hands, with Prince Charles, at the head of the Duchy of Cornwall, the largest single landowner.

Reaching 2,000ft (600m), the moor is the highest land in southern England, and generates a climate of its own. Around half of it is open moorland, and the rest (particularly on the eastern side) is steep wooded valleys with secluded villages.

In the distant past the climate was kinder, and the high moor was more heavily cultivated and populated than it is today. The first people worked the moor 10,000 years ago, and 7,000 years ago it was mostly covered in trees. But as the climate worsened, so the population left their dwellings in search of easier ground lower down. As a result Dartmoor has a wealth of Bronze Age sites – around 2,000 – dating from around 4,000BC; hut circles, tombs and ceremonial stones. But not every interesting-looking stone is man's creation: centuries of frosts have cracked the granite into what look like intentional shapes particularly on the tors (derived from the same root as 'tower').

Mixed in with Bronze Age remnants are signs of more recent industry, in particular the mining of tin, granite and copper from the 12th to 19th centuries. Tin mining – largely tin streaming in the open river beds – was a boom industry, and the Dartmoor miners were granted special

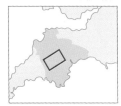

Watch out for the wildlife

exemption from the nation's taxes. Although they never numbered more than a few hundred, they made a powerful group with their own laws, their own parliament (which met at Crockern Tor) and their own judiciary and prison at Lydford. Their contribution to the nation's coffers was made at the strategically placed stannary towns of Ashburton, Chagford, Plympton and Tavistock; here the tin was weighed and duty paid.

Strange legends and traditions persist, including the pastime of letterboxing, a sort of moorland treasure hunt (*see page 69*), and even as recently as the mid-19th century, if you could build a house on Dartmoor between sunrise and sunset, then it and the land became yours.

Some areas of moorland have been designated for military use since the Napoleonic Wars. On firing days warning flags fly around the restricted areas, and post offices and visitor centres display details of firing schedules.

The eastern gateway to the moor is the small town of **Bovey Tracey**, whose long main street begins to climb the hillside. It was the scene of an undignified fracas during the Civil War when royalists were surprised at cards, but the former managed to escape by scattering their stake money, which proved too much of a temptation for the poor Cromwellians.

39

Bovey's solid granite architecture is unremarkable, but it does have two shopping highlights. **Teign Valley Glass** (in a small industrial estate on the Exeter side of town) has glass and pottery in a synthesis of museum and retailing, with limited glass-blowing on site. Proceed further towards the centre of town and you will reach the ★ **Devon Guild of Craftsmen**, located in an appealing old riverside 'mill' (actually a stable block with a waterwheel to pump water to the horses), and with exhibition space on the first floor. The range and quality of the Devon Guild's members is extremely high, but prices can be steep.

Traditional arts and crafts

From Bovey head west towards Widecombe. Just outside town is **Parke House**, the headquarters of the Dartmoor National Park Authority. There are some pleasant walks in the grounds, but the Parke Rare Breeds Farm is no longer.

At this point a short diversion northwest towards Manaton brings you to ★ **Becka Falls**, actually more a dramatic series of tumbles than a waterfall, with tea-room and nature trails in very pleasant woodland.

Meanwhile the Widecombe road climbs steeply, and the moor opens out at the very popular ★★ **Hay Tor** (1,491ft/ 450m), with far-reaching views. It is a short and relatively easy walk from the road to the rocks. Running along the back shoulder of the hill is the **Granite Tramway**, which is as it sounds: a track made from granite, complete with

Becka Falls

points, which was used to transport granite from the gash of a quarry in the hillside 10 miles (16km) down to the Stover canal. The tramway may look as old as the hills, but actually it was constructed in 1820. The quarry became uneconomic after 30 years, but its stone travelled far and wide, and was used in London Bridge.

To the northwest is **Hound Tor**, and in the valley on the far side are the clear remains of a medieval village amongst the bracken.

Tea stop in Widecombe

Widecombe-in-the-Moor, a small, captivating place superbly situated in a deep trough which is nevertheless still 800ft/240m above sea level, has become something of a tourist mecca thanks to the song about its annual fair which immortalised several local names. The song dates from the 1860s, and was intended as advertising to attract Uncle Tom Cobley and all away from similar events. Such is the power of advertising that the fair remains a major celebration (second Tuesday in September), featuring country skills and crafts.

Widecombe's church

Widecombe's other claim to fame is its church, known as the **cathedral of the moor** because of its tall tower. It sits beside the pretty village green, but its main pathway leads in from the gate next to the old parish hall, now a National Trust property with a shop. Its interior is plain and broad, and on the wall inside the entrance is the sombre description of how lightning struck in 1638 during a service, and four people were killed.

Down narrow lanes south of Widecombe are two other pretty Dartmoor villages. **Buckland-in-the-Moor**, although scattered around a wooded hillside, has one of the most photographed groups of thatched cottages in Devon. The small church has an unusual clockface boasting the words MY DEAR MOTHER instead of numerals. South still is **Holne**, birthplace of author Charles Kingsley. The 14th-century Church House Inn is one of Dartmoor's most characterful.

From Widecombe the main road heads west through the surprisingly popular spot of Dartmeet (see Postbridge for a better-preserved clapper bridge), and thence up to Two Bridges. Both locations are little more than their names suggest: the former is the meeting place for the East and West Dart rivers, and the latter is a hotel next to old and new river crossings.

Another dappled day

Princetown, the highest and bleakest settlement on Dartmoor sheltering beneath the huge transmitter mast on North Hessary Tor, has the grim aspect of a frontier town, and is regularly cut off. Amazingly, a railway reached here from Plymouth in 1883, but was closed in 1956.

After the mast, the town's landmark is **Dartmoor**

Prison, which was built in 1806 for French prisoners of the Napoleonic Wars. After the introduction of deportation to the colonies it actually stood empty for many years, but today it functions as one of Britain's maximum security jails. A small **museum** charts its history, and gathers together some confiscated items over the years. Its manager must be the only museum curator in the country liable to be called away in the event of prison riots.

Just by Princetown's central crossroads is the ★★ **High Moorland Visitor Centre**, with well-presented displays on Dartmoor's history and wildlife and insights into some of its legends. This is also the place to find out about the schedule of guided walks.

Across the road is the ancient **Plume of Feathers**, the oldest building in the area (1795). During a refreshment stop here, you can ponder the story of the fearful winter wayfarer who opened a box seat in his room to discover the body of a man. Murder was assumed, until the landlord confessed that the body was that of his father, and he was only being stored there while the ground remained too hard to be dug.

From Princetown return east to Two Bridges and turn north for **Postbridge**. This straight stretch of road has perpetuated one of Dartmoor's best known legends – that of the hairy hand, reputed to have caused several accidents by appearing from nowhere and wresting control of the steering wheel. The clapper bridge at Postbridge is the best preserved on the moor.

Postbridge in winter

The moor gradually softens as the road continues northeast, finally arriving in the heart of **Moretonhampstead**, a potentially attractive small town which is rather blighted by the five roads that meet in the town centre. With nearby Chagford, Moreton has become something of an arts and crafts centre. The church lies on the west side of the town; at its Cross Street entrance stands a beech tree on a raised stone circle. This so-called 'dancing tree' replaces an ancient elm which had dancing platforms in its branches. On the way out of town are Moreton's dour **almshouses**, dating from 1637 and the property of the National Trust.

Sign of times past in Moretonhampstead

Chagford lies a short distance north, off the A382 to Okehampton. Its stannary past has left the town looking remarkably elegant, gathered around a small market square at the centre of which is the six-sided and spired Market House (1862) known locally as the Pepperpot. Shopping around the square is a mixture of hardware and arts and crafts. Off the top left-hand corner of the square is the 16th-century Three Crowns hotel, where Cromwellian soldiers had a brief encounter with royalists during the Civil War. The Three Crowns looks out over the graveyard and the 15th-century granite church of St Michael.

Castle Drogo's gardens

Back on the road to Okehampton, motorists will soon be aware of the silhouette of ★★ **Castle Drogo** (April to October, daily except Friday, 11am–5.30pm; National Trust) up on the hill to the right, although the journey to its door is some miles through narrow lanes. This dramatic situation was chosen by one Julius Drewe whilst picnicking here with his family. Drewe, who had made his fortune in retailing, recruited the architect Lutyens, bought a nearby granite quarry, and thus the last castle to be built in England was begun in 1910.

It was finished some 20 years later in much truncated form. Drewe's enthusiasm had long since evaporated, partly because of the death of his son – with whom he had conceived the project – in World War I. Although the property was given to the National Trust in 1974, the latest generation of Drewes is still in residence.

Castle Drogo has plenty of features, including a wonderful bath, a dedicated power generating system, and tapestries that date from the 16th century. Outside are terraced gardens in yew hedges and woodland walks down into the Teign gorge. Particularly worthwhile is the walk to **Fingle Bridge**, a 400-year-old footbridge of some charm a couple of miles upstream, which can also be reached by road via the pretty hilltop village of **Drewsteignton**.

Finch Foundry

Just before Okehampton, in Sticklepath, is the ★ **Finch Foundry** (April to October, daily except Tuesdays, 11am–5.30pm; National Trust). The most remarkable thing about this forge was that it was still manufacturing edged tools by hand as recently as 1960, using hammers, shears and grindstones powered by waterwheels – all still in working order. Local farmers swear by their Finch tools.

The new A30 sweeps past the market town of **Okehampton**, cutting it off from the moor to which it spiritually belongs. Okehampton is a matter-of-fact sort of place, and is particularly well-served by the ★★ **Museum of Dartmoor Life** (daily 10am–5pm, weekdays only in winter) through an arch just off the main street. The museum gives detailed but visitor-friendly insights into the archaeology and sociology of the moor, with good use of aerial photography.

Museum exhibit

Okehampton's ★★ **Castle** (April to September, daily 10am–6pm) has been a ruin since Henry VIII seized it in 1538, but what it lacks in roof it makes up for in location, on a hilltop in a wooded valley half a mile behind the museum, and with a riverside picnic area below. The castle was built in 1068 by Baldwin de Brionne, the first sheriff of Devon. It served primarily as a family house, but the thick-walled keep is the best preserved of the buildings.

To complete this route, return to the A30 and then take the moor-skirting A386. Half way to Tavistock, just off to the right, is the village of **Lydford**, a former administrative centre of the Royal Forest of Dartmoor whose castle is actually just a prison keep, but with earth thrown up around it to give it the appearance of a castle. From 1200 Lydford was the site of the stannary court, and by all accounts Lydford law was particularly severe: 'in the morn they hang and draw and sit in judgement after'. These days you will find a far warmer welcome in the Castle Inn next door.

The scenic ★ **Lydford Gorge** (National Trust) is just beyond the village. The river Lyd thunders through it, shadowed by an alarming walkway. In more gentle scenery downstream the river is joined by the elegant White Lady Waterfall, which is actually more a slide than a fall.

Lydford Gorge

The last stop on this route, ★★ **Brent Tor**, can be reached either via back lanes from Lydford or by returning to the A386. Either way, the tor with the church of **St Michael de Rupe** perched on its summit is visible from some distance, rising dramatically out of gentler fields to a height of 1,100ft (330m), with stunning all-round views. The rock is thought to be the lava plug of a volcano which has since crumbled away. The first church was built here in 1130, but the present simple and solid building is 13th century.

43

Legend has it that the church was originally built at the bottom of the hill, but the devil transported the stones to the top in the belief that the climb would deter worshippers. Every Sunday a small congregation proves the devil wrong.

From here it is a short distance to Tavistock, described in *Route 5, see page 37.*

St Michael de Rupe, Brent Tor

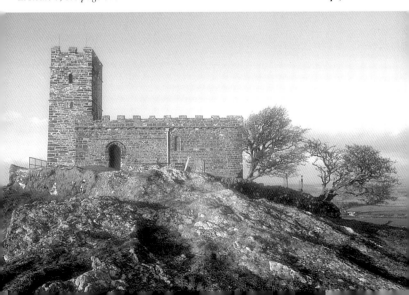

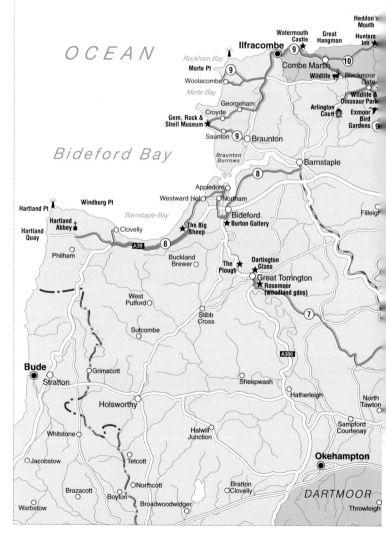

**ROUTES 7–10
MID & NORTH DEVON**

0 ____ 10 km
0 ____ 5 miles

N

ATLANTIC

OCEAN

Rockham Bay

Ilfracombe

Heddon's Mouth

Watermouth Castle Great Hangman Hunters Inn ★

⑨ ★

⑩

Morte Pt

⑨

Combe Martin

Wildlife ★ Blackmoor Gate

Woolacombe

Morte Bay

Georgeham

Croyde

Wildlife & Dinosaur Park

Gem, Rock & Shell Museum ★

Saunton ⑨ ○ **Braunton**

Arlington Court

Exmoor Bird Gardens ⑨

Braunton Burrows

○ **Barnstaple** ⑧

Bideford Bay

Appledore ○

Hartland Pt

Windburg Pt

Westward Ho! ○ Northam

Barnstaple Bay

Hartland Abbey �

○ Clovelly ★ **The Big Sheep**

Bideford ★ **Burton Gallery**

Filleigh

Hartland Quay

A39 ⑧

Philham ○

Buckland Brewer ○

The Plough ★ Dartington Glass ★

Great Torrington **Rosemoor** ★ (woodland gdns)

West Putford ○

Stibb Cross ○

Sutcombe ○

A386 ⑦

Bude ●
Stratton

○ Grimscott

Sheepwash ○

Hatherleigh ○

North Tawton ○

Holsworthy ○

Sampford Courtenay ○

Whitstone ○

Halwill Junction ○

○ Jacobstow

Tetcott ○

Bratton Clovelly ○

Okehampton ●

Brazacott ○

○ Northcott

Boyton ○ Broadwoodwidger ○

DARTMOOR

Warbstow ○

Throwleigh ○

44

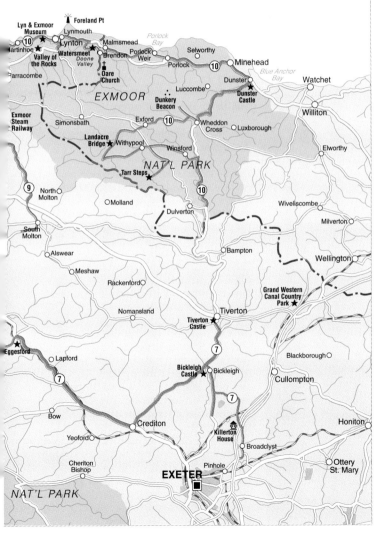

Route 7

Mid-Devon and Tarka Country

Killerton – Bickleigh – Tiverton – Eggesford – Great Torrington *See map, p44–5*

Devon's holiday industry has traditionally centred on the two coasts and to a lesser extent the moors, ignoring the great swathe of land in-between. But Mid-Devon is a green and pleasant land, and in these environmentally-conscious days its store is slowly increasing. There are no major towns here, just rolling fields and scattered villages, but that's the region's charm.

Having said that, the first section of this route, from Exeter to Tiverton, is a bit of an exception. Carrying the West Country's major road and rail links, this short stretch also hosts several fine country houses.

Killerton House

After its grand parkland approach, one's first impressions of ★ **Killerton House** (April to October, daily except Tuesday, 11am–5.30pm; National Trust) is that it is rather small and unimpressive given the huge estate it governs. In fact Killerton, which was built by the Acland family in 1778, was only intended as a temporary residence while something rather grander was in mind. In the event, such plans were abandoned.

The house interiors are interesting, if unexceptional, and the first floor hosts the National Trust's costume collection, with new displays every year. Much of the pleasure of Killerton, however, lies in the gardens, which extend up the hill behind, and include an ice-house and a charming summerhouse known as the Bear's Hut, after the family pet which was kept here.

Killerton was given to the National Trust in 1944 by Sir Richard Acland, who felt that his ownership of 17,000 acres (6,880 hectares) was incompatible with his position as leader of his own Common Wealth party. At the time, the Trust only had three members of staff, and Killerton became its largest property. Estate houses are lime-washed a distinctive yellow.

Closer to Tiverton, ★ **Bickleigh Castle** (May to October, daily except Saturday, 2–5.30pm, guided tours) is still in private hands. It is a great deal older than Killerton, and its 900-year-old chapel is said to be the oldest complete building in Devon, even surviving a period as a cowshed. The resident Carews took the Royalist side in the Civil War, and accordingly their castle was greatly diminished by the victorious parliamentarians (Cromwell was here in 1646), and only the gatehouse remains from the original 14th-century establishment. The main accommodation is a farmhouse added in 1650, and a cluster of thatched outhouses around a pleasant courtyard, one of which now includes an eccentric museum.

Bickleigh cottage

Bickleigh itself is much photographed as the typical Devon village, particularly the thatched cottages by the river Exe next to the 16th-century bridge.

47

Upstream, **Tiverton** is a matter-of-fact town, divided by an unappealing stretch of the river Exe, alongside which stands Heathcoat's Textile Factory, a reminder of the town's past success in the woollen and latterly lacemaking trade. Its pannier market is hidden apologetically in the middle of a central square on the east bank.

Down St Andrew Street, in an old school beyond the barn-like St George's Church, is the **Tiverton Museum** (February to December, daily except Sunday, 10.30am–4.30pm), an emporium of local relics, including such prizes as the door of the prison and a turnip cutting machine. Its most famous exhibit is the Tivvy Bumper, a tank engine that once ran on the Exe valley railway,which is housed in its own shed.

Tiverton

Returning to St George's, St Peter's Street leads up to the church of the same name, and just beyond that stands **Tiverton Castle**, also diminished after suffering much the same fate as Bickleigh, and still lived in.

An interesting feature of Tiverton is the recently-created **Grand Western Canal Country Park**, on an 11-mile (18-km) stretch of canal dating back to 1810 which was part of a grand design to cross the West Country from sea to sea. Construction proceeded piecemeal – and then the railways arrived. Today the Country Park has its beginning in an unlikely suburban setting southeast of the town centre, and trips by horse-drawn barge are available in summer months.

From Tiverton, return to Bickleigh and take the road to Crediton, and don't hurry: the views from this hill road can be excellent. Turn north onto the A377 at Crediton and you are entering what has recently been designated Tarka Country, after Henry Williamson's book *Tarka the Otter*. The long-distance footpath the Tarka Trail kicks off at **Eggesford station** for its 180-mile (288-km) meander through deepest Devon.

Eggesford's All Saints Church

That Eggesford was once part of a big estate is evidenced in the 14th-century ★ **All Saints Church**, in a pastoral setting on the valley slope. Within are ancient family tombs of the Chichesters, Fellowes and Copplestones, all of whom have Eggesford connections. The original big house was on the site now occupied by the **Garden Centre**, which has a display on Tarka Country and a lovely view from the tea-room. More recently, a bigger mansion was built up on the hillside to the north, but it was sold for £7,000 in 1914, and left to decay, although its facade is still highly visible. Rumour has it that one room was found to have been papered in penny black stamps, but they were too much damaged to have any value.

Eggesford is surrounded by mature woods with way-marked walks and cycle trails.

Down a country lane

From here, leave the beaten track and plunge west to pick up the road to Torrington. There's a choice of two routes, equally scenic, although the villages on the A386 are the more interesting. Worth a detour is **Hatherleigh**, newly bypassed. Here a couple of ancient thatched hostelries – the George Hotel and the Tally Ho!, the latter with its own brewery – are complemented by a studio pottery with African designs.

Rosemoor, under the eye of hill-top Torrington, is a large garden with visitor centre presently being developed by the Royal Horticultural Society, following the donation of the grounds of Rosemoor House by Lady Anne Berry in 1988. Unless you are a plant enthusiast, then the most pleasant area is Lady Anne's Garden, around the original house – sadly at the far end of the development.

It is easy to miss the best of **Great Torrington**, slicing through its rather drab outskirts on the road to the coast. The old town – recorded in the Domesday Book of 1086 – is tucked around a little square with the town hall at its centre. At one side is the **Plough**, a popular arts space, but the striking success story is ★ **Dartington Glass** which was also set up by the Elmhirsts and now employs 300 people and exports worldwide. The factory includes a visitor centre and guided tour of the factory on aerial walkways (weekdays only, 9.30am–4pm), which gives the glassmakers an opportunity for a bit of showmanship.

From here it is a short drive to Bideford, and *Route 8*.

Route 8

Barnstaple

North Devon

**Barnstaple – Bideford – Lundy – Westward Ho! –
Clovelly – Hartland** *See map, p44–5*

The arrival of the A361 linking North Devon with the
M5 at Tiverton has provided a welcome economic boost
to the region, and nowhere more so than at **Barnstaple**
(pop. 25,000), a farming town where industrial estates and
shopping centres have bloomed in the new spring.

Barnstaple has a very long history. Pilton, a district to
the west of the centre, received its royal charter in 930,
making it one of the oldest burghs in England. The town's
early success was due to its position at the highest navigable and lowest crossable point of the river Taw, but then
the silting up of the river and the growth of Bideford put
paid to serious trade. The town's strategic position was
highlighted again at the beginning of the railway age when
five lines converged here, of which only one remains. And
now the new road brings another resurgence.

Barnstaple Junction in the 1960s

Little remains of Barnstaple's origins. The Norman Castle, near the Civic Centre, is just a mound spiked with trees.
The first bridge was built in 1273, and although it has been
much altered since, you can still see the original brickwork
if you take the riverside underpass at the east end.

A focal point of Barnstaple on Tuesdays and Fridays
is the ★★ **Pannier Market**, on the High Street, in a building which dates from 1855. This is the best of Devon's
many such markets. Produce is also on sale throughout the
week in Butcher's Row, a colourful parade of shops that
runs along the market flank.

Under one roof: the market

Penetrate through a narrow lane halfway down
Butcher's Row and you enter a hidden, grassy square with

Queen Anne's Walk
The Queen's Head public house

the unexceptional St Peter's Church to the right and the graceful **St Anne's Chapel** (1330) in the centre. The chapel has had many functions, and once housed the grammar school attended by poet John Gay.

The centre of town rather ignores Barnstaple's **Square**, with its Albert Memorial Clock, but don't miss the new ★★ **Museum** (daily except Sunday, 10am–4pm), next to the bridge. Hands-on displays highlight wildlife, sea-life, transport, industry (especially pottery, *see below*), folklore, etc of the area in an excellent, compact collection.

Just downriver from the square is the colonnaded **Queen Anne's Walk** (1709), where merchants gathered to do their deals with the figure of the queen above their heads. Upriver from the square, up Litchdon Street, are the **Penrose Almhouses** (1627), and if you linger within the quad one of the residents might give you a tour of what he gets for £30 per week. Barnstaple's remaining commercial pottery, **Brannams** (weekdays, 10am–4.15pm) is on the Bideford side of the town, and visitors are given the chance to throw their own pots.

Continue out on the Bideford road, which eventually leaves the Taw estuary and swings left to meet the Torridge. Across the water are views of first Appledore, with its covered shipyard, and then **Bideford** itself, with a jumble of houses and shops behind a pretty riverside quay. The new link road bridge, high overhead, has released the pressure on Bideford's 24-arch bridge, much of which dates from 1535, but the quay remains the focus of town life. Bideford was once the third largest port in Devon, and ships left here for the Americas, although shallow waters restricted significant later development and today most of the space is taken by fishing boats and leisure craft.

At the far end of the Bideford quay is Victoria Park, and the ★ **Burton Gallery** (daily, 10am–5pm), a new arts space of great distinction, with a small museum upstairs.

The quay is also the mainland station for ★★ **Lundy Island**, a lonely, peaceful 3-mile (5-km) slice of high land 11 miles (18km) offshore. Lundy is owned by the National Trust and managed by the Landmark Trust, and is rich in curiosities and natural history. The resident population is well outnumbered by 35 puffins.

The *MS Oldenburg* sails to Lundy from Bideford up to five times a week in summer. There's a pub, shop and a variety of accommodation (including the old lighthouse). For information, tel: (01237) 470422.

Appledore is still fundamentally a fishing and boat-building village, with close-packed white cottages climbing the hill, and a small seasonal **maritime museum** up above, from where there are tremendous estuary views.

On a bench in Bideford

Around the corner facing the open sea is the Victorian resort town of **Westward Ho!**, which borrowed its name from the epic novel by Charles Kingsley based on Bideford, where Kingsley was living in the 1850s. The resort was created by a 19th-century development company who realised the potential of two miles of sandy beach and extensive grasslands of Northam Burrows.

Westward Ho!

One of the most innovative of Devon's farm attractions is the ★ **Big Sheep** at Abbotsham, just off the A39. Anything to do with sheep takes place here – lamb-feeding, shearing, sheepdog trials and even sheep racing.

The A39 shadows the coast to just above ★★ **Clovelly**, a perfectly preserved fishing village, which flows like spilt paint down a steep hill to a small harbour. Clovelly was unknown until 1850, and is still privately owned by descendants of the Hamlyn family, who live in Clovelly Court at the top of the hill. The temptation to get the most out of tourism has been restrained to the new visitor centre by the car park. Below it the village is remarkably unspoiled, even down to the rather uncomfortable cobbles (there is an alternative Landrover service in season).

Cobbled Clovelly

51

Most of the village income is derived from its 300,000 annual visitors, although fishing boats do still function. Charles Kingsley lived here, while his father was curate at the church, and a small Kingsley museum is adjacent to a preserved fisherman's cottage. The Clovelly lifeboat is still active, and it too has a small museum.

This is undoubtedly a treacherous coast for ships, and nowhere more so than off **Hartland Point**, the last stop on this route. This is Devon's coast at its most wild.

Hartland has a wilder image

Hartland's layout has been determined by the weather. Its lighthouse is right on the point, while the village, with a long, low main street, is a couple of miles inland. The manorial residence of **Hartland Abbey** (the abbey remains date from 1157, main house from 1779, access limited to Wednesdays and Sundays in summer) is tucked into a sheltered valley below the village of Stoke, on the way to Hartland Quay. The Stucley family who still own Hartland Abbey also have their own side chapel in **St Nectan's** church up above, which has the tallest tower (128ft/38m) in North Devon. St Nectan's bears the marks of its exposed position. Note the counterweighted church gate.

From here it is a short descent to ★★ **Hartland Quay**, which these days is little more than a hotel clinging to some of the finest cliff scenery in Britain. The quay was authorised by act of Parliament back in 1586, and it was still functioning until the end of the 19th century, since when storms have smashed it to smithereens. This is a strikingly beautiful place, backed by massive cliffs with muscular veined strata, and likely to leave a lasting impression on the visitor who comes here on a stormy day.

Route 9

East of Barnstaple

Braunton – Woolacombe – Ilfracombe – Combe Martin – South Molton *See map, p44–5*

A day on the beach

The best of North Devon's beaches are just to the west of Barnstaple. En route is **Braunton**, where surf shops give a clue of what is to come. The flat land to the left of the road is more interesting than it seems; what used to be RAF Chivenor is now a base for the Royal Marines, and beyond it is the Braunton Great Field, an ancient field system with divisions still visible. Penetrate down these lanes to ★ **Braunton Burrows**, sand dunes known for their botany and bird life, with views over the estuary.

Most visitors continue on to **Saunton**, an impressive stretch of beach, popular with land-yachts, wind- and wave-surfers, although with limited access thanks to the golf club, which stretches along its back.

The road girdles the headland to **Croyde Bay**, with holiday camps and an attractive beach. In the pretty village is the **Gem, Rock and Shell Museum**, essentially an expanded shop reflecting the enthusiasm of the family who run it. Ask to see the meteorite and cross-section of agate with million-year-old water trapped inside.

Georgeham church

Take the right turn up through the village and on via a narrow road to **Georgeham**, shoe-horned into a narrow valley. Henry Williamson wrote *Tarka the Otter* here.

Woolacombe's famous sands

From here, ★ **Woolacombe**, the finest beach in Devon, is tantalisingly close, but hard to reach. Penetrate north through lanes and you will reach the former railway station, now reborn as a children's attraction called Once Upon a Time. Turn left, and the road descends gradually to the beach below. The beauty of Woolacombe is the uniform sand, the dunes and the green sward behind them.

On non-beach days a fine alternative is to round the corner to Mortehoe, park the car and walk to ★ **Morte Point** on a grassy headland with great cliff scenery.

The major resort of the north is **Ilfracombe**, although it lacks a beach of quality. It started out as a fishing village in the 19th century, but its natural harbour brought steamer traffic and the railway. The tide of tourism rose quickly, and the population had doubled by 1860, and doubled again by 1891. But the high water mark was reached, and the tide has since receded in other directions, leaving the town rather fossilised somewhere between then and now.

Its location is good, and its unprepossessing main street is up the hill away from the main tourism area, preserving the holiday enclave, to which three small shoreline hills provide shelter. The most seaward (Lantern Hill) protects the characterful ★ **port**. Lundy trips, sea fishing charters and coastal cruises aboard a paddle-steamer are offered here. Lantern Hill is crowned by **St Nicholas Chapel**, with neat whitewashed interior and all-round view.

At the foot of the third shoreline hill is the eccentric ★ **Museum** (10am–12.30 in winter, 10am–5.30pm April to September). The collection charts the resort's heyday and includes plenty of oddities: a drawer full of old wedding cake, a two-headed kitten, and the complete Ilfracombe radio station. A hundred yards west, and the best of Ilfracombe's beaches can be reached (for a fee) via a tunnel through the foot of the hill.

Ilfracombe's port

The road east out of Ilfracombe rolls around the coast. It plunges down to sea level at **Watermouth Cove**, with a natural harbour. Watermouth Castle has been converted into a children's playland.

Little Hangman rises steeply out of the sea on the far side of the bay of **Combe Martin**. There are fine walks up to the peak from the carpark, and thence onto the shoulder of Great Hangman. Combe Martin's most unusual building is the **Pack of Cards** public house, built by a gambler to resemble just that, with 52 windows and 52 doors.

Little Hangman

At the top of the valley is the ★ **Wildlife and Dinosaur Park** (Easter to end October, 10–4pm), one of the premier attractions in the region, with full-size dinosaur models in the woods, miniature railway, falconry displays, etc.

The A399 climbs inland, onto the fringes of Exmoor. Off to the right is ★★ **Arlington Court** (April to October, daily except Saturday, 11am–5.30pm; National Trust), North Devon's only substantial country house open to the public. Arlington is not particularly old (built in 1822) or grand, but it is imprinted with the character of its most recent owner, Rosalie Chichester, a grand dame and collector, and has the added attraction of magnificent parkland (including a heronry).

Also worth a detour, on the other side of the A399, is the tiny church of ★ **St Petrock**, on the upper edge of the nestled village of Parracombe. Parts of this church may be 13th century, but its uniqueness lies in the fact that it has been supplanted by a newer church, and thus remains a relic of the 18th century, complete with hand-lettered scriptures on the screen, rickety pews and planking. In winter the key is available from a house just up the lane.

The A399 runs along the edge of the moor, with fine views off to the left, past the **Exmoor Bird Gardens** and **Exmoor Steam Railway**, before dipping down into the lush Bray valley, and thence to **South Molton**, a pleasant Georgian market town known for its antiques shopping. From here it's a quick journey back to Barnstaple, or on to Tiverton.

Route 10

Exmoor

Lynmouth – Doone Valley – Selworthy – Dunster – Dulverton *See map, p44–5*

At 265 sq. miles (670 sq. km), Exmoor is the second smallest of Britain's National Parks, but contains an incredible variety of landscape and wildlife. Parts of it are open heather-covered moor, but the park (of which a quarter is in Devon and the rest in Somerset) also includes some of Britain's most dramatic and beautiful coastline – which forms a major part of this route.

Exmoor is lower than Dartmoor and its landscape rather more gradual. It is more extensively farmed and habitation is more widespread. Its Bronze Age remains are not so good, although Tarr Steps is finer than any clapper bridge found on Dartmoor. Many hills are topped by Iron Age forts or Beaker period barrows, but although Edward II licensed a local lord to dig six of the latter, they yielded nothing. Much of this landscape is celebrated in the most famous tale from either moor, *Lorna Doone*.

54 *Exmoor explorations*

This route begins from Combe Martin, at the western edge of Exmoor. Be warned: the first section follows the dramatic coastline through steep and difficult roads, of which the first is a taste of what's to come: Shute Lane leaves Combe Martin's main street just down from the Pack of Cards, and rapidly climbs to such a height that Dartmoor can sometimes be seen on a clear day, to the south. On the left of the road is ★★ **Great Hangman**, reached by footpath, with breathtaking cliff scenery.

After a couple of miles running parallel with the valley of Combe Martin, turn left at a junction signed to Trentishoe and Hunter's Inn. Shortly after the turning you'll pass the National Park sign. Here, too, the views continue, with the vale of Parracombe dropping down to the right, and the barren 1,146-ft (344-m) **Holdstone Down** with fine walking and cliff scenery rising up to the left.

The road then slips inland to descend into the thickly wooded Heddon valley. At the bottom, the half-timbered ★ **Hunter's Inn** is a popular refreshment stop and focal point for walks, notably down the bubbling Heddon to Heddon's Mouth, a stony cove with a kiln once used to process lime shipped here from Wales, for use as fertiliser.

Take the steep road alongside the inn signed to Martinhoe, and then go left towards Woody Bay at the next T junction. The road soon starts to descend through hanging oak, and the scattered houses of Woody Bay become visible, like limpets on the hillside. In Victorian times, an entrepreneur tried to turn Woody Bay into a resort, and built a pier which has since gone. A few hotels remain. Following signs to Lynton, take the toll road up through the Lee Abbey estate. In fact abbey is a misnomer; the building has never been such, although it is home to a Christian community. You should now be looking down into the **Valley of the Rocks**, a dramatic land formation thought to have been created by the river Lyn. Legends link the devil with the valley's formation.

The road climbs out of the valley and into the back of **Lynton**, another Victorian development. George Newnes, publisher of the Sherlock Holmes stories, gave the town its grand town hall, where the tourist information office is located. Take a right down into Queen Street for the heart of the town. Round the corner at the bottom is the seasonal **Lyn and Exmoor Museum**, in a cob cottage.

Newnes also financed the building of the ★★ **Cliff Railway** (daily 8am–7pm), which links Lynton with Lynmouth, 500ft (150m) below. The railway is worked by water. The car at the bottom discharges its 700 gallons until the weight of the top car is sufficient to pull it to the top. In the early days of motoring, before good brakes, it sometimes carried vehicles.

On the Cliff Railway

Lynmouth's main attraction is its location. Its small harbour is guarded by the Rhenish Tower. The Cliff Railway arrives on the seafront almost next to the **Exmoor Visitor Centre and Lifeboat Museum**. Lynmouth's history has two dramatic episodes. The first is the epic story of how, in 1899, when a ship got into trouble off Porlock Weir, the sea was too wild to launch the Lynmouth Lifeboat, so instead it was dragged up Countisbury hill and across country to Porlock. The second is the savage flood of 1952, when 9 inches (23cms) of rain fell in 24 hours, and 90 million tons of water came crashing down the Lyn gorge, killing 34 people and altering the face of the town.

Lynmouth

The gorge contains some dramatic rocky riverscapes, and is well footpathed – although the lower stretches are less interesting. ★ **Watersmeet**, a 19th-century fishing lodge turned into a tea-room and shop (National Trust), is a good place to start, and from here you should walk upstream. Years ago this dramatic scenery was used in cigarette advertising, with the slogan 'Cool as a mountain stream'. Walk up the East Lyn river and you'll emerge at Brendon, on the doorstep of the ★★ **Doone Valley**.

To travel to the valley by car, leave Lynmouth on the Porlock road up Countisbury Hill – marvelling at the feat of pulling the lifeboat all this way – and once past County Gate (you are entering Somerset) take a right signed to Brendon. Turn left at the bottom for Malmsmead, and the pretty, winding valley climbs gradually into bandit

THE LORNA DOONE HOTEL & RESTAURANT OPEN TO NON-RESIDENTS

country, marked by the attractive little **Robber's Bridge**.

The actual story of R D Blackmore's *Lorna Doone* has become less well-known than the region itself (for a precis, *see page 60*). Suffice it to say for the moment that Lorna was an unwitting heiress, kidnapped by outlaws who lived on the moor, and rescued by a local hero. In fact, the 'real' Doone Valley lies a little further west, but this whole region counts as Doone country.

Lorna and her hero were married in **Oare Church**, where Blackmore's grandfather was vicar. It is worth penetrating up to **Malmsmead**, with its 17th-century bridge and ford, and walking alongside the river up to Cloud Farm, where you can usually get a cream tea as reward.

Return to the A39, and descend (the toll road has better views) to **Porlock**. The flat valley bed indicates how far the sea has receded, because Porlock once had a port, since relocated to Porlock Weir. The town itself is pretty, and well-stocked with shops. The 13th-century St Dubricius – named after the Welsh missionary who supposedly married King Arthur and Guinevere – is unusual, with its rich interior and truncated spire. From Porlock Weir, it

Culbone Church

is well worth the 1¼-mile (2-km) walk along a lovely section of the coastal path to the remote ★ **Culbone Church**. With sections dating from the 11th century, it is said to be the smallest complete parish church in England.

Real picture-book prettiness is to be found a little further on, in ★★ **Selworthy**. The village was part of the

Selworthy cobhouse

Killerton estate (*see page 46*) which explains why the cob houses are a uniform yellow. All Saints Church (14th-century) is a dramatic white, with views out over the valley and up to Dunkery Beacon (*see below*). Inside, look for the local aristocrats' balcony pew over the porch.

Continue on to **Dunster**, a well-preserved medieval town with a dramatic 19th-century ★★ **Castle** (April to October, Saturday to Wednesday, 11am–5pm) and 17th-century circular ★ **Yarn Market**. Because of its many attractions and its location next to Minehead, Dunster is on the coach tour route, and there's lots to see.

Yarn Market

This route, however, is concentrating on Exmoor, and this is where it turns inland, up the A396. After some miles turn right at Wheddon Cross, towards Exford. If the day is clear, branch right to ★ **Dunkery Beacon**, Exmoor's highest spot at 1,704ft (511m). The Beacon rises gradually, the walk is easy, and from the top one can supposedly see 16 counties.

Exford, sheltering in the Exe valley, is considered the heart of Exmoor. It has been the home of the Devon & Somerset Stag Hounds since 1875, and they can often be heard baying in the distance. The 15th-century church of **St Mary Magdalen**, above the village, has the stalk of an ancient cross outside, and a 500-year-old screen re-located from Watchet. Its list of rectors dates back to 1297.

The village is a centre for Exmoor recreation, and from it roads spread in several directions. Cross the river bridge and turn left up the hill. At the top, go straight over the crossroads, through a ford and eventually to ★ **Landacre Bridge**. This striking medieval structure is in a superb situation on the river Barle; desperately lonely in winter, it is very popular with picnickers in summer. It's a fine walk upstream to the Iron Age fort at Cow Castle, and thence to the well-situated hamlet of **Simonsbath**, former nerve centre of the Royal Forest and another Exmoor crossroads.

Cross Landacre, climb out of the valley and turn left to the village of **Withypool**, which also has a grand old bridge, but the ultimate in old river crossings is further still: climb out of Withypool and turn right at the cross-roads. The road runs along the wild back of Winsford Hill, with fine views. Eventually you'll come to a right turning signed ★★ **Tarr Steps**. Descend to the car park and walk down to this 17-span clapper bridge, said to be up to 3,000 years old. It looks immaculate, but it has been washed away by floods three times this century and had to be rebuilt. The riverside walks are excellent.

Back up on Winsford Hill, retrace your steps a mile or so and take a right down into the pretty village of **Winsford**, dominated by the Royal Oak Inn. Streams run through the village to the extent that there are seven bridges within a matter of yards of each other.

The A396 runs to the east of Winsford. Head south, and turn off it at the signpost for **Dulverton**. This handsome farming town on the river Barle is the headquarters of the National Park, has an Exmoor Visitor Centre in the new library on the main square, and a heritage centre in the Guildhall just behind. It's a good place to research anything that has caught your interest about Exmoor.

Tarr Steps

57

Dulverton's Exmoor Visitor Centre
Landacre Bridge

A Writer's Devon

Devon features extensively in the nation's literature, although not always to its favour. The county's own home-grown collection of literary figures is eminent enough (Charles Kingsley, Samuel Taylor Coleridge, Agatha Christie, R D Blackmore, John Gay), but many more giants of literature came here seeking inspiration; literary giants need holidays, too.

Some of these visitors borrowed Devon locations and traditions. Conan Doyle, for example, visited Dartmoor, and used the name of his coachman-guide – Baskerville – in his fictional account of Sir Richard Cabell of Buckfastleigh, the *Hound of the Baskervilles*. Rudyard Kipling based *Stalky and Co* on his experiences while at the United Services College in Bideford. Anthony Trollope described a thinly-disguised Tavistock in his book the *Three Clerks*, and Charles Dickens set one of the scenes from *Pickwick Papers* in Exeter's Turk's Head (next to the Guildhall), still serving in Dickensian surroundings today.

Conan Doyle

Anthony Trollope

59

Other writers and poets simply used Devon as a peaceful place for the creative process. Evelyn Waugh wrote *Brideshead Revisited* while staying in a hotel near Chagford. John Galsworthy wrote the *Forsyte Saga* while living on a farm at Manaton, on the eastern side of Dartmoor.

Percy Bysshe Shelley was in full flow in Lynmouth – but then he was in something of a romantic whirl at the time, having just run away with a 16-year-old girl and married her, against her parents' wishes.

Evelyn Waugh

Not everyone was kind about the gentle countryside around them. Jane Austen pokes fun at Dawlish (which she visited on holiday) in *Sense and Sensibility*. Poet John Keats got bored in Teignmouth, where his brother Tom was sent to recuperate, but at least he was relatively polite about it in his letters.

Less diplomatic was fellow poet Robert Herrick. Writing of his period as vicar of Dean Prior in the 17th century, Herrick said:

'More discontents I never had
Since I was born, than here;
Where I have been, and still are sad,
In this dull Devon-shire.'

Judging by the quality of this piece, the county certainly didn't inspire him to create great poetry.

A more sinister side of life in Devon is captured by some of the late poems of Sylvia Plath, who together with Ted Hughes (a poet usually associated with Yorkshire) lived in a thatched vicarage near Okehampton for a time. Plath was both drawn and repelled by cosy, picturesque Devon.

Though she embraced local country pursuits – bee-keeping, riding, picking blackberries, attending Evensong – for her they served only to accentuate bleaker, more unsettling aspects of nature.

In tourism terms, the biggest impact has been made by Henry Williamson, who was not native to Devon but came to settle in Georgeham, near Croyde, on the north coast, where he worked in a shed that he built in the middle of a field with the proceeds from a literary prize. His are the most telling footprints on the Devon landscape, thanks to his book *Tarka the Otter*, and to a lesser extent *Salar the Salmon*. Devon County Council has christened much of Mid Devon Tarka Country, and various key points along the Tarka Trail are directly associated with events in the book.

Second to these books is R D Blackmore's *Lorna Doone*, an epic set in the 17th century which has given a new label to the upper East Lyn – the Doone Valley. Blackmore, who wrote part of the book while staying in the Royal Oak in Winsford, actually had the valley of Lank Combe in mind as the home of his outlaw family, the Doones (based on the original Exmoor outlaws, the Gubbins), although the Malmsmead valley has since taken over the title. Snippets of the Doone story are associated with many places, but the whole story is seldom told. For the sake of context, a short precis follows:

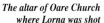

Doone Valley

60

The altar of Oare Church where Lorna was shot

The Doones were originally outlaws from Scotland who settled on Exmoor and terrorised travellers and locals. At a lonely spot on the moor a local boy, John Ridd, whose honourable father had been killed by Carver Doone, by accident met and fell in love with the Doones' supposed daughter, Lorna. She appeared to be a prisoner to her own family. By this time the Doones' activities had outraged

national sentiment, and a strong army force was sent out to find and destroy them. John Ridd, hearing of this expedition, feared for Lorna's life, and crept into the Doone valley under cover of night to spirit her away. Carver Doone – the man who killed John Ridd's father – came after the couple. Lorna turned out not to be a Doone at all, but the heir to a noble estate in Scotland which was to have been claimed by the Doones through the marriage between Carver and Lorna. John Ridd and Lorna get married in Oare Church, but Carver shoots Lorna at the altar. John Ridd chases him onto the moor, and a hand to hand fight ensues in which Carver is finally swallowed up by a peat bog. John returns to find Lorna only slightly wounded, and all live happily ever after.

Also a strong crowd-puller – even bringing the Japanese to Torquay – is Britain's most prolific author, Agatha Christie, who still sells a massive 4 million copies a year worldwide. Agatha Christie was born in Torquay in 1890, and spent much of her lifetime in the area. She wrote two of her books while staying in the Art Deco hotel on Burgh Island. Her house, Greenway, on the banks of the Dart, is pointed out by all the pleasure boat captains, although it is hard to see through the trees. It is still lived in by her daughter, and is opened to the public on rare occasions. There are permanent exhibitions devoted to the writer in Torre Abbey and the Torquay museum.

Robber Bridge

Agatha Christie, born in Torquay

Charles Kingsley, author of the *Water Babies*, was born in the Dartmoor village of Holne, although he is more closely associated with the North Devon coast, particularly Clovelly, where his father was vicar, and Bideford, where the name of the local resort *Westward Ho!* is derived from one of his books (with his approval). It is a singular honour – the only place name in the UK to be derived from a book title, and to include an exclamation mark.

Samuel Taylor Coleridge was born in Ottery St Mary, where his father was rector, and although he spent most of his life elsewhere, he never lost his Devon accent. In later years Southey and Coleridge would carouse in the Ship Inn on the waterfront at Porlock Weir; and it was an unknown person from Porlock who so rudely interrupted Coleridge's poetic fantasy *Kubla Khan*.

John Gay, poet and author of the *Beggar's Opera*, was born in Barnstaple, and went to school in the charismatic small St Anne's Chapel, where a small exhibition preserves some of the atmosphere of the time.

These days Devon's most famous living author is its independent-minded Conservative MP for Torbay, Rupert Allason, writing spy thrillers under the pen-name Nigel West. Who knows – there may be other, still greater figures out there now, but only time will bring them forward.

'Typical' Devon

The rural idyll

Wherever you go in Devon, you will inevitably find yourself in a 'typical' village. Many lay claim to the title of Devon's most typical, but in effect each area has something different to recommend it. On anyone's list of top villages you are likely to find Clovelly, Bickleigh, Cockington, Chagford, Buckland-in-the-Moor, Widecombe-in-the-Moor, Branscombe, and others besides.

But this is a county of villages, every one of which is typical; even Devon's chief city, Exeter, has a villagey feel. Its biggest conurbation, Plymouth, is the exception that proves the rule, but Plymouth belongs more to the sea than the land. The rest of this third largest county in the kingdom is largely given over to small communities, in a landscape of irregular sloping fields threaded by narrow lanes. Take any of those narrow lanes and inevitably you'll reach a small, isolated church, probably Norman in origin, a couple of shops and a pub.

This sparse and scattered Devon landscape is largely the result of its social structure. It has long been a county of small farmers (average holding 65 hectares), 60 percent of whom are owner-occupiers, which is a high proportion in national terms. The county was never dominated by wealthy families, so there are few large estates. It is a land of self-contained communities, with their own building materials, strong accents and interests. Within these communities a scattering of professional people have a semi-feudal status: the vicar, the doctor and the headmaster are the holy trinity.

Markets and mines

Past lives

Many of Devon's towns are extended villages which benefited from the siting of farmer's livestock and pannier markets. All over the county farmers' wives used to bring in their home produce once a week and sell it from makeshift stalls. Today the finest of these markets is held at Barnstaple on Tuesdays and Fridays, but most towns still have functioning pannier markets, and Totnes even stages a weekly market in Elizabethan dress in summer.

A few towns, particularly around Dartmoor, were the creation of the mining industry, and are usually distinguished by rather more imposing architecture such as at Ashburton and Tavistock, as a sign of the wealth the industry produced. Miners would trek into these towns to have their tin or copper weighed, certified and sold.

A characteristic of the modern Devon landscape is the 'farm park'. As agriculture has become increasingly unviable for small farmers, so they have turned to tourism. Rare breeds farms, wildlife parks, bird sanctuaries, specialist pony centres, etc are common everywhere.

Local names and architecture

Local communities have local names, often including topographical features such as oak, ash, wood or marsh, and ending in -cott or -worthy. Many include the word combe meaning valley. Barton is an old word for farm; tor, prevalent around Dartmoor, means hill; around Exmoor the equivalent is moel, meaning upland, which emerges in various forms such as the river Mole or the village of Molland. Many main streets are called Fore Street, and some of the older towns have a Butterwalk (pillared section of pavement) or a Shambles, such as at Totnes and Dartmouth. Building materials were often very local; the churches of central Devon reflect the redness of the soil (especially around Crediton), whilst many in the southeast are made from Beer limestone.

Along the steep and narrow

Many thousands of Devon's distinctive whitewashed cottages, with rounded, bulging and uneven walls, are made from cob, a homespun mixture of clay, stones, straw, hair and cow dung. Until 150 years ago cob was the most popular building material across the county, and it lasts forever provided it is kept dry and allowed to breathe. Should moisture accumulate within it, however, it is likely to return to the earth from which it came. Devon's most recent cob structure – a bus shelter – was built in the 1970s, but the practise has largely faded into history.

63

Strangled by charm

Devon's charming topography, which was once enormously beneficial to local industry, providing streams for mills and creeks for boats, has proved economically frustrating in the modern era. Navigable rivers and hidden coves were excellent for the small boat and small trade period; towns of the south coast such as Totnes, Colyton, Otterton and Topsham profited from being tucked away inland, safe from pirate raids. But then boats grew bigger, rivers silted up, and their trade disappeared.

Change has come slowly to Devon. A couple of the water-powered corn mills – at Hele near Ilfracombe and at Otterton in East Devon – are still grinding, and the water-powered Finch foundry, near Okehampton, was still hand-forging edge tools until 1960. Such places close one day as businesses, and open the next as museums.

Setting a slow pace

For the tourist, the advantage of all this is that much of Devon has been fossilised; everyone can find their own corner and mine it for its nuggets of traditional gold, be they in local festivals, local brews or the contents of the local antique shop.

Tourism destroys, but it also preserves, and Devon's traditional qualities are increasingly appreciated. Fine examples can be seen in the Devon Guild of Craftsmen at Bovey Tracy, where local skills are reaching new markets.

Food and Drink

Opposite: a Devonshire cream tea

The food industry has a long tradition in Devon, dating back to the days when the ports were in their prime and flotillas needed provisioning. This tradition, combined with a scattered local population, has kept the supermarket culture at bay, and Devon is one of a decreasing number of regions where small town centres still have thriving markets, shops, and even traditional grocers.

But although the quality of local Devon food is good, this is not the county for *haute cuisine*. Good, substantial farm fare is typical, and is particularly available in local pubs, delicatessens and markets. Outside Plymouth and Exeter top quality restaurants find it a struggle to survive: instead, select hotels such as Gidleigh Park and Whitechapel Manor specialise in gastronomic getaways.

The huge Devonshire Cream Tea business is serviced by a large number of local dairies – but it wasn't always thus. Devonshire clotted cream was first celebrated in the 14th century, but it became almost a forgotten memory until tourism reintroduced that delicious glue between scone and jam.

65

Country pubs abound

The dairies also produce a wide variety of local cheeses, not produced in sufficient quantities to enter supermarkets, but regularly stocked in delicatessens and in pannier markets. Many hotel restaurants support the local producers. The Ticklemore Cheese Shop in Totnes has a good cross-section of Ticklemore's own, as well as cheeses from other producers. The Big Sheep (*see page 51*) is a substantial cheese producer as well as a family tourist attraction, and plans are afoot to initiate a food village on the site.

Devon's final dairy speciality is ice-cream, usually available in resorts. Look out for Langworthy's in Dartmouth, Rocombe's in Torquay, Thorne's in Ilfracombe. At Salcombe you can watch it being made in the shop in Shadycombe Road, or buy it direct from the farm shop at Langage, Plympton.

Fruit and fish

Devon is rich in pick-your-own fruit farms and accompanying preserves, cordials and fruit wines. Buckfast Abbey and the Quince Honey Farm of South Molton are both known for their honey, and Quince encourages visitors to view its bees going about their sticky business.

Cider apples (which are rather more bitter than table apples) grow everywhere, and some rural pubs serve a local scrumpy drawn from a barrel under the bar. Scrumpy can be an acquired taste, and packs a considerable punch. There are plenty of cider makers whose brands – such as the memorable Old Pig Squeal produced near Totnes –

Try the local cider

Can't be better than in Brixham

make it into local shops and pubs. Hancocks near South Molton welcomes visitors to its charming, rather tumbledown cider-making centre, where business and pleasure mix together.

Grapes grow well in the south, with vineyards at Down St Mary (near Crediton), Loddiswell (near Kingsbridge), and in a lovely location down to the shores of the Dart at Sharpham (Ashprington, near Dartmouth). Nearby is the Blackawton brewery. Tucker's Maltings, in Newton Abbot, is the only traditional malthouse (turning barley into malt for beer) in England open to the public.

The fishing industry is still important in the south, so menus are strong on seafood. Local specialities to look out for are Brixham plaice, Dartmouth dressed crab and Salcombe smokies (smoked mackerel).

Markets and bakeries

There's a strong trade in home-made produce at most pannier markets. Look out for quality baking, as well as chutneys, mustards, marmalades and preserves of every kind. One of the best locations is Barnstaple market on Friday, alongside the Butcher's Row line of shops. In the south, there's a fine selection of local foodstuffs at the Dartington Cider Press Centre (*see page 29*).

High Street bakeries are generally excellent. Although pasties were invented for the Cornish miners, they have gained wide acceptance in Devon as a midday meal. Many bakeries receive overnight deliveries from Cornwall.

For anyone really interested in local foods, there are two key annual events: the Festival of West Country Food and Drink (Exeter) in March, and Feast (Totnes) in June.

Further details of local producers are available from Taste of the West, Agriculture House, Pynes Hill, Rydon Lane, Exeter, EX2 5ST, tel: (01392) 445675

Tea on the terrace and ices on the prom

Restaurants

Price categories (based on three-courses, per person, without wine): **£££** = £35 or more, **££** = £20, **£** = up to £20.

Barnstaple

££Lynwood House, Bishop's Tawton Road, tel: (01271) 43695. Town house restaurant with accommodation. Long-standing reputation amongst the locals.

Bideford

£Hoops Inn, tel: (01237) 4512220. Long, low thatched pub on the A39 between Bideford and Clovelly. Real ale and good seafood. Accommodation available.

Chagford

£££Gidleigh Park, tel: (01647) 432367. Gastronomy at a price, on the connoisseurs' and celebrities' circuit.

Dartmouth

£The Dolphin, Market Square, tel: (01803) 833835. A pillared, tile-clad characterful old pub that specialises in local fish: scallops, mussels and Dartmouth dressed crab.

£Billy Budd's, 7 Foss St, tel: (01803) 834842. Seaside bistro with honest fish and imaginative meats: try the seafood crêpes and the lamb with chilli and ginger.

Dulverton

£Tarr Farm, Tarr Steps, tel: (01643) 851383. 16th-century farm converted to restaurant and tea-room. Right next to the ancient clapper bridge. Traditional cooking.

Dunster

£Tea Shoppe Restaurant, 3 High St, tel: (01643) 821304. Ancient cottage. Traditional menu based on local produce.

Lynmouth

££The Rising Sun, Harbourside, tel: (01598) 753223. Well known locally for its high standards. Simple menu focusing on local game and seafood.

Moretonhampstead

£The Reverend Woodforde, Cross St, tel: (01647) 40691. Small restaurant with short menu featuring fresh, French cuisine with a strong emphasis on herbs.

Plymouth

££Piermasters, Southside St, tel: (01752) 229345. Fish specialities and French cuisine with herbs in good location in the heart of the Barbican.

Sherford

£Stancombe Cyder Press, tel: (01548) 531151. Tiny restaurant in thatched 16th-century apple store, hidden in the south Devon lanes. Satisfying farm cuisine.

South Molton

£££Whitechapel Manor, tel: (01769) 573377. Elizabethan Manor House, high quality cuisine, local produce.

Withypool

££The Royal Oak, tel: (01643) 83506. Not to be confused with the more striking Royal Oak in Winsford, this country hotel has a first rate restaurant in traditional style.

Old-fashioned service

67

Mountain biking on Exmoor
Welcome to Dartmoor

Active Holidays

Devon is a county for **walking**. Its most famous long-distance routes are the Templer Way, Two Moors Way, Tarka Trail, and the South West coast path. Both moors have guided walks, organised by the National Parks themselves and usually with a ranger as guide. Dartmoor hosts the annual Ten Tors Expedition, in which young people orienteer themselves across the moor via 10 selected peaks.

Some walks have also been designated **cycleways**, but mountain bikers are particularly asked to stick to the agreed routes. Bikes can be hired throughout the county. For a useful booklet, *Walking and Cycling in Devon,* describing the major walks, and giving details of cycle hire opportunities, contact Devon Tourism, tel: (01392) 383260.

There is excellent **white water canoeing** on the river Dart, and to a lesser extent the Barle and the Exe. Such canoeing has to be done outside the fishing season, of course – but anyway these are fast-flowing rivers, quickly affected by rain, which would be barely navigable in summer.

A well-trodden path

A couple of the river estuaries – notably the Dart and the creek at Salcombe – have **summer canoeing**. The Tamar is navigable for a long way, winter and summer: Tamar Canoe Expedition, no experience necessary, tel: (01579) 351113. **Sea-canoeing** takes place along the south coast, the north coast being too treacherous for most forms of small boating. South coast centres are Dartmouth and Salcombe, where craft can be hired.

Horse riding is popular on both moors. On Exmoor try Knowle Riding Centre, tel. (01643) 841342; Brendon Manor Farm, tel: (015987) 246; Hawthorne Stables, tel: (01643) 831401. On Dartmoor try Eastlake, tel: (01837) 52513; Lydford House, tel: (01822) 820347.

For those who like horses but prefer to do their riding

on wheels, Arlington Court now offers carriage driving lessons from novice level upward, in the lovely setting of the Arlington grounds, tel: (01271) 850296.

The moors were originally designated Royal Parks for the purpose of hunting, shooting and fishing. **Shooting** still takes place on both moors and Exmoor hosts the largest commercial pheasant shoot in the country. Exmoor also has plenty of deer where Dartmoor has practically none, and hosts three **staghunts**.

Game fishing for trout is popular on the fringes of both moors. Local hotels usually have fishing rights, or can make arrangements for guests. In addition, the Exe, the Torridge, the Taw, the Tamar and the Dart are salmon rivers. Local hotels such as the Rising Sun at Umberleigh are popular with salmon fishermen.

Sea-fishing can be productive, but less so from the shore than from a boat. Many fishermen make a good income from taking out fishing parties in the summer.

Catch as catch can

Dartmoor has something of a unique activity in its **letterboxing**. Some 2,000 'letterboxes', usually tin boxes, are hidden in remote locations over the moor. Walkers search out a particular letterbox (they get the location from another letterboxer, or the letterboxing newsletter), stamp their own book with the letterbox's stamp, and then head on for the next. This occupation is so popular that an estimated 1,000 letterboxers take to the moor every weekend. For information, tel: (0154882) 1325.

69

Beaches

Broadly speaking, there are around 70 recognised beaches in the county, of which around three-quarters are in the south (the north makes up in quality and space what it may lack in quantity). Most of these beaches are sand, although sometimes this may mean sand at low tide only.

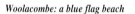

Woolacombe: a blue flag beach

Three South Devon beaches have blue flag awards for beach management and water quality: Meadfoot, Broadsands and Oddicombe, all in the Torbay area. In East Devon, the most striking strand is Exmouth, while to the west of Torbay, the beaches to look out for are Blackpool Sands, East Portlemouth to Salcombe South Sands in the Salcombe creek, Hope Cove, Bigbury and Thurlestone.

Up in the north, dune-backed Woolacombe is the blue flag beach, and is the finest in the county. Nearby Saunton Sands runs it a close second, and between the two Croyde is also popular, although tides here can produce swirly currents. There are a few hidden coves worth seeking out, notably Sandy Cove between Ilfracombe and Combe Martin. Be prepared for a long descent!

For a more detailed assessment of individual beaches and their facilities, contact Devon Tourism for their Devon Beach Guide, tel: (01392) 383260.

Getting There

By car

Most car travellers arrive in Devon via the M5 motorway, which is fed by the M4 from London (roughly 200 miles/320km) and the M6 from the north. Travellers from southern England wishing to avoid the motorway should take the A303 to Taunton. The M5 sweeps around Taunton and enters the county near Tiverton, before joining the A30 just outside Exeter and thundering on through South Devon. Access to North Devon is via the A361 link road, which leaves the M5 near Tiverton and strikes across country to Barnstaple. Other roads into the county are scenic, but slow.

By coach

Direct long distance express coaches operate to Devon from most areas. National Express has regular services into Plymouth, Torbay, Exeter, and North Devon from London, the Midlands and the North. For information tel: (0990) 808080.

71

By train

Exeter is served by fast trains (less than 3 hours) from Paddington, some of which also stop at Tiverton Parkway (NB this is largely a commuter stop, and is some distance from the town). An alternative London service (Regional Railways) runs from Waterloo, via Hampshire and Dorset, but takes a little longer. There are also direct services (Cross Country) from the north via Bristol. For information on all services contact National Rail Enquiries, tel: (01752) 221300.

Two ways to travel

There are many different kinds of tickets available, depending on the degree of flexibility you require, and it is worth researching your options in advance (be sure to be clear about exclusions). The cheapest tickets currently available, offering considerable savings on both normal returns and 'Saver' tickets, are Apex. These are subject to availability, must be booked at least seven days in advance, can only be used on the trains specified at the time of booking and the return journey must be made within one calendar month.

By air

Both Exeter and Plymouth have airports. Scheduled services operate to Exeter from Manchester, Belfast, Dublin, Cork, the Channel Islands, Morlaix and Amsterdam, Brussels and Paris. Airport information, tel: (01392) 367433.

There are also scheduled services into Plymouth from Heathrow, Cork, Dublin, Bristol and the Channel Islands. Airport information, tel: (01752) 772752.

Getting Around

Devon is a large county with few major transport arteries. Public transport is widespread, but so is the population, so don't expect to get anywhere in a hurry. Bus travel can nevertheless be quite an adventure. Schedules tend to vary according to local market days and to seasons; because of their height above sea level, Dartmoor and Exmoor can be inaccessible due to weather conditions in winter.

Making friends on Dartmoor

Driving

It's a sadly undeniable fact that, if you're not a walker or a cyclist, a car is the best method of exploring the county. However many city drivers can make fools of themselves in the country lanes, losing their nerve in narrow stretches and getting stuck on steep hills, of which there are plenty. Allow double time for all car journeys, and don't try to hurry. Devon's roads were not built for speed, and there's likely to be a tractor, herd of cows, or caravan somewhere just ahead. Be particularly vigilant on the A361 North Devon link road, where the two/three lane system has produced some crazy driving, and several bad accidents.

Follow that sign

City centre parking is, by national standards, quite good in Devon. Exeter has several multi-storey car parks – imaginatively decorated with murals – within easy walking distance of the town centre, as well as outlying park-and-ride locations. Plymouth is a little more difficult, and public transport is advisable into the town centre, although there's lots of metered parking around the Hoe. Most other locations have pay and display car parks. Please use them – Devon's streets and lanes are narrow enough without illegally-parked vehicles increasing the problem.

In general it is always good to know the market days of your local town, because these greatly affect the amount of traffic making its way to the centre.

Car rental

All major companies have offices in both Plymouth and Exeter.
Avis, tel: (01392) 59713
Budget, tel: (01392) 496555
Eurodollar, tel: (01392) 50858
Hertz, tel: (01392) 57791

Rail connections

From Exeter (St Davids) regional connections run to Barnstaple and Exmouth, and from Newton Abbot to Paignton. From Plymouth, a service runs up the Tamar Valley to Gunnislake. Information, tel: (01752) 221300.

Very popular preserved steam railways link in with British Rail at Paignton (to Kingswear), tel: (01803)

Crossing the River Dart

555872 and at Totnes (to Buckfastleigh), tel: (01364) 642338. Both of these services are seasonal, however. The only winter services are Santa Specials, at Christmas.

Bus routes

The local bus network is extensive, and transport guides are available for four regions: North Devon, East Devon, Mid Devon and Dartmoor. Notable services are the Transmoor Link, which links Exeter and Plymouth across Dartmoor National Park, the Moorland Motor Coach, a 1950s classic bus which runs between Okehampton and Moretonhampstead on summer Sundays, and the Bike Bus, running between Exeter, Okehampton and North Devon, with capacity for six bicycles. Devon Bus enquiries, tel: (01392) or (01752) or (01271) 382800.

Boat connections

Three scheduled passenger-carrying ferries still operate from Devon's coasts, all year round. Two car and one passenger ferry make the short crossing across the Dart, between Dartmouth and Kingswear; Brittany Ferries sail from Plymouth to Spain; and the *MS Oldenburg* runs between Lundy Island, Bideford and Ilfracombe, with one month's pause for a refit in winter.

Otherwise there are several excellent areas for boat trips. On the south coast, Tor Bay (usually Torquay to Brixham), the river Dart estuary up to Totnes, connecting one steam railway with another, the creek from Salcombe to Kingsbridge and Plymouth Sound and Harbour are all well served by regular sightseeing cruises. On the north coast, Ilfracombe is the base for seasonal trips, in particular with *Waverley* and *Balmoral* period steamers. Furthermore most seaside towns with harbours offer some sort of small scale boat trips either for sightseeing or fishing. Contact local tourism offices for details.

A fun day out

Dusk falls on Torquay

Facts for the Visitor

Tourist information

The county is well served with tourist information centres (TICs), of which the smaller ones may well only be open in the season. For general tourist information on the county as a whole, tel: (01392) 437581. For information on Tor Bay (Torquay, Paignton and Brixham), tel: (01803) 296296. For information on Mid Devon, the Tarka Country Tourism Association is on tel: (01837) 83399. For Lundy Island, tel: (01237) 470422.

Other TICs are as follows:
Axminster, tel: (01297) 34386
Barnstaple, tel: (01271) 388583
Bideford, tel: (01237) 477676
Brixham, tel: (01803) 852861
Budleigh Salterton, tel: (01395) 445275
Combe Martin, tel: (01271) 883319

Keep in touch

Dartmouth, tel: (01803) 834224
Dawlish, tel: (01626) 863589
Exeter, tel: (01392) 265700
Exmouth, tel: (01395) 222299
Honiton, tel: (01404) 43716
Ilfracombe, tel: (01271) 863001
Ivybridge, tel: (01752) 897035
Kingsbridge, tel: (01548) 853195
Lynton, tel: (01598) 752225
Newton Abbot, tel: (01626) 67494
Okehampton, tel: (01837) 53020
Ottery St Mary, tel: (01404) 813964
Paignton, tel: (01803) 558383
Plymouth, tel: (01752) 264849
Salcombe, tel: (01548) 843927

Seaton, tel: (01297) 21660
Sidmouth, tel: (01395) 516441
South Molton, tel: (01769) 574122
Tavistock, tel: (01822) 612938
Teignmouth, tel: (01626) 779769
Tiverton, tel: (01884) 255827
Torquay, tel: (01803) 297428
Totnes, tel: (01803) 863168
Woolacombe, tel: (01271) 870553

In addition, the **National Parks** have their own information centres:
Dartmoor, tel: (01626) 832093
Exmoor, tel: (01398) 323665

    The National Trust and **English Heritage** have a variety of properties around the county, many of which are included in the text of this book. For overall information, contact their regional offices: National Trust, tel: (01392) 881691. English Heritage, tel: (0171) 973 3434.

Familiar guardian
A walk in Exmoor Park

Guide services
City
Red Jacket guides of Exeter, tel: (01392) 265212, have free city tours. Blue badge guides in Plymouth can gain access to areas otherwise closed: Armada Guides, tel: (01752) 402879, or Guides Southwest, tel: (01752) 667790.

Rural
Dartmoor Safaris, tel: (01364) 661514. Dartmoor guided walks, tel: (01822) 890414. Exmoor guided walks, tel: (01398) 23841. Horsedrawn Tours, Exmoor, tel: (01598) 752310.

Rivers
Dart Pleasure Craft, tel: (01803) 834488.

Disabled
For local information on accommodation, places to eat etc, and hire of disability aids, contact Holiday Services for Disabled Holidaymakers and their Families, Teignmouth, tel: (01626) 779424.

    For advice on special needs transport, contact the Transport Co-ordination Centre, County Hall, Exeter, tel: (01392) 382123.

    Regional advice for the disabled: in East Devon, tel: (01395) 516551, ext. 373. In the South Hams, tel: (01803) 866519. In Plymouth, tel: (01752) 600633. In North Devon, tel: (01271) 25888.

    Health on Call, for 24-hour non-emergency health care and advice, tel: (0891) 517766. Also has hire of equipment and information on doctors, dentists and chemists on call.

For Children

*Necessary tools
At the Donkey Sanctuary*

Of the beaches, those at Paignton (Goodrington Sands and Paignton Green), Exmouth and Teignmouth in the south, and Westward Ho!, Saunton and Woolacombe in the north have the best combination of quality sand, space and accessible facilities. The southern beaches are more crowded, thanks to their urban setting and sheltered climate.

As mentioned elsewhere in this book, Devon's farmers have been innovative in diversifying into the tourist business, usually with some sort of farm park, where cuddling, feeding or riding animals are encouraged. Such attractions are too numerous to detail here, but worth picking out are the Sidmouth Donkey Sanctuary, the Shire Horse Centre (near Plymouth), the Big Sheep (near Bideford), Bodstone Barton, Combe Martin Wildlife and Dinosaur Park, and Watermouth Castle (all near Combe Martin).

There are miniature railways in East Devon at Beer's Pecorama and Bicton Park; in North Devon at Great Torrington (near Rosemoor Gardens) and the Exmoor Steam Railway, near Bratton Fleming; in South Devon at Gorse Blossom and Trago Mills (near Newton Abbot).

In Exeter, the Connections Discovery Centre has particular attractions for children. In Plymouth, the Dome will grip them with its moving history, and the same could be said for Morwellham Quay, up the Tamar Valley. In Torquay, Bygones and the Babbacombe Model Village are well-established favourites, as is the innovative Paignton Zoo. Brixham has the Deep, an underwater fantasyland, and a replica of the Golden Hind. The North Devon Museum in Barnstaple is very rewarding for the curious-minded child.

Child's play, Torquay

Accommodation

Farm stays
Devon Farms collates a wide range of both bed and break-fast and self-catering accommodation right across the county. Tel: (01548) 550312 for a brochure.

Self-catering cottages
This is a boom market for Devon. In addition to the big national letting agencies, there are a number of regional specialists:

West Country Cottages, tel: (01626) 333678
Helpful Holidays (Chagford), tel: (01647) 433593
Beach and Bracken Holidays (Bratton Fleming), tel: (01598) 710702
Coast and Country Cottages (Salcombe), tel: (01548) 843773
Farm & Cottage Holidays (Bideford), tel: (01237) 479698
Toad Hall Cottages (Kingsbridge), tel: (01548) 853089
Marsdens Cottage Holidays (Braunton), tel: (01271) 813777
North Devon Holiday Homes (Barnstaple), tel: (01271) 76322

Why not hire a cottage?

Hostels, camping barns and camp sites
There are 13 YHA youth hostels in the county, including on Dartmoor, Exmoor, Exeter and Plymouth. Tel: (01722) 337515, for details.

Camping barns, or 'stone tents', are a relatively new concept across Devon and owned by individual farmers, but co-ordinated by the YHA. Barns vary, but showers and cooking facilities are standard. Many are located on long-distance footpaths and cycle trails. Tel: (01271) 24420.

Holiday camps, caravan sites and camping facilities are widespread, particularly in coastal areas. Ask local TICs for details.

The English Riviera
Accommodation possibilities in the Torbay area are too numerous to mention here. Contact the Riviera tourist board, tel: (01803) 296296, for their guide.

A grander option, Torquay

Hotels
Price categories, per person per night: **£££** = £60 *or more,* **££** = £30–60, **£** = *up to £30*

Branscombe, East Devon
£££Bovey House Hotel, tel: (01297) 680241. 12th-century country house hotel with 9 bedrooms, excellent restaurant. Fine rural location.

Bigbury on Sea

£££Burgh Island, tel: (01548) 810514. Unusual Art Deco hotel on an island first inhabited in AD900 by monks, with access by sea tractor. Agatha Christie wrote two books here. Smart clientele which dresses up for dinner.

Chagford

£Three Crowns Hotel, tel: (01647) 433444. 13th-century inn with a colourful history in prime location in one of Dartmoor's most attractive small towns.

Combe Martin

££Sandy Cove Hotel, Old Coast Road, tel: (01271) 882243. Family hotel with spectacular outlook over the bay. Swimming pool can be covered or uncovered.

Dartmouth

Royal Castle, Dartmouth

££Royal Castle Hotel, The Quay, tel: (01803) 833033. Former 17th-century coaching inn on the quay. A focus of the town's social scene, with lively bars and good food.

Dulverton

£The Lion Hotel, Bank Square, tel: (01398) 323444. Traditional-style old town hotel, right in the centre of Dulverton. Its restaurant has a reputation for good food.

Exeter

££Royal Clarence Hotel, Cathedral Yard, tel: (01392) 319955. Imposing, historic hotel, opened in 1769, great views over the cathedral close. *££The White Hart Hotel*, South Street, tel: (01392) 79897. Situated just below the cathedral, it is a rambling 15th-century coaching inn, arranged around a courtyard. Lots of atmosphere.

Exford

££White Horse Inn, tel: (01643) 831229. Imposing 16th-century inn right in the middle of Exmoor.

Holne, near Ashburton

£Church House Inn, tel: (01364) 631208. 14th-century inn in small village on the eastern slopes of Dartmoor, with good access to major Devon routes. Excellent food.

Lynmouth

Lynmouth's Rising Sun

££The Rising Sun, Harbourside, tel: (01598) 753223. A group of 14th-century cottages (a smuggler's inn, it is thought) strung together by the water. Quality restaurant.

Plymouth

£££The Grand Hotel, The Hoe, tel: (01752) 661195. Victorian property with history in great location overlooking the Hoe. Geared towards a business clientele.

Princetown

£Plume of Feathers, tel: (01822) 890240. Oldest building (1795) on the high moor, with lots of character and a variety of accommodation, from bunk house to en suite.

Winsford, Somerset

£££The Royal Oak Hotel, tel: (01643) 851455. Very upmarket, very attractive thatched hotel in the middle of the moor.

Index